# APRIL

## A MONTH OF IDEAS AT YOUR FINGERTIPS!

### PRESCHOOL–KINDERGARTEN

## WRITTEN BY

Barbara Backer, Jan Brennan, Diane Gilliam, Linda Gordetsky, Ada Hanley Goren, Lucia Kemp Henry, Lori Kent, Angie Kutzer, Carrie Lacher, Linda Ludlow, Suzanne Moore, Sharon Murphy, Vicki Pacchetti, Mackie Rhodes

## EDITED BY

Lynn Bemer Coble, Ada Hanley Goren, Jennifer Rudisill, Gina Sutphin

## ILLUSTRATED BY

Jennifer Tipton Bennett, Cathy Spangler Bruce, Pam Crane, Clevell Harris, Lucia Kemp Henry, Susan Hodnett, Sheila Krill, Rob Mayworth, Rebecca Saunders, Barry Slate, Donna K. Teal

## TYPESET BY

Lynette Maxwell

## COVER DESIGNED BY

Jennifer Tipton Bennett

www.themailbox.com

©1996 by THE EDUCATION CENTER, INC.
All rights reserved.

ISBN# 1-56234-152-9

**Manufactured in the United States**
10 9 8 7 6 5 4

# TABLE OF CONTENTS

# April Calendar

## Keep America Beautiful Month

April is the time to focus on keeping our planet green and clean. Involve your class in this worthy cause by selecting a project to beautify your school or center grounds. Have children plant flowers or start a recycling bin. Present each youngster with a packet of flower seeds to take home and encourage her to spread the message—Keep America Beautiful!

## International Guitar Month

Help celebrate the tribute to the guitar this month with a hands-on experience. If possible, let students hold a guitar and experiment by strumming and plucking its strings. Have each student make his own guitar by stretching several rubber bands around a shoebox. Then strike up the band as students play along to various recordings of country, jazz, and classical guitar tunes.

## Listening Awareness Month

Sharpen listening skills this month by focusing on stories, songs, and games that involve a variety of sounds. These "sound-sational" titles will have youngsters all ears: *Joe Joe* by Mary Serfozo (Margaret K. McElderry Books), *The Noise Lullaby* by Jacqueline K. Ogburn (Lothrop, Lee and Shepard Books), and *Say Please* by Virginia Austin (Candlewick Press).

## Month Of The Young Child

Started in Michigan, this focus promotes the importance of young children and their needs. Many communities celebrate with special events for children and families. Let your little ones know how special they are with a party in their honor. Plan a celebration with tasty treats, photos of everyone's brightest smile, and a parade around the playground. Conclude the event by awarding certificates recognizing each student's best quality.

*(Turn the page for more…)*

## 2—Birthdate Of Hans Christian Andersen

With more than 150 fairy tales to his credit, Hans Christian Andersen is an outstanding figure in children's literature. Celebrate the anniversary of his birthdate by reading such classics as *The Princess And The Pea*, *The Ugly Duckling,* and *The Emperor's New Clothes*. After sharing several of Andersen's stories, ask youngsters to vote for their favorite. Create a class graph to show the results.

## 7—World Health Day

The World Health Organization established this day in 1948 to remind people of good health habits. Each year, a different theme for good health is highlighted. For information on the current theme, write to: World Health Day, American Association For World Health, 1129 20th Street NW, Suite 400, Washington, DC, 20036. Then reinforce healthy habits by having your students pantomime ways to take good care of themselves. Set the motions to music as you incorporate their actions sung to the tune of "Here We Go 'Round The Mulberry Bush." "This is the way we brush our teeth, brush our teeth, brush our teeth…!"

## 21—Kindergarten Day

Celebrate Kindergarten Day on the birthdate of its founder, Friedrich Froebel, who established the first kindergarten in Germany in 1837. The idea was introduced to America by German immigrants, and by 1873, the first public kindergarten opened in St. Louis, Missouri. Ask upcoming kindergartners to discuss their feelings about entering kindergarten. Ask your seasoned kindergartners to recall their favorite activity or special event from the year.

## 22—Earth Day

The original Earth Day, held in 1970, called attention to the need of purifying our air, land, and water. Have your youngsters explore the creatures that make their homes in each environment. Label three charts with the titles "Air," "Land," and "Water." Have students look through magazines to find examples of life in each area. Then discuss the importance of keeping each habitat clean. Conclude by having students paint pictures of happy creatures in healthy environments. (For more activities related to Earth Day, see the unit on pages 66–75.)

## 26—National Arbor Day (Last Friday In April)

Although some states observe this event on different dates, April is traditionally the month to honor trees. Make students aware of the importance of trees for food, shade, habitats, lumber, and landscaping purposes. Take your students outdoors to sit under a tree as you share a "tree-mendous" tale, such as Shel Silverstein's *The Giving Tree* (HarperCollins Children's Books).

# April

## CLASSROOM NEWS

Teacher: _____ Date: _____

## A Peek At The Week

## Looking Ahead

## Reminders

## Help Wanted

## Special Thanks

# Our Need For Seeds

Dig into this cross-curricular unit and uncover the magic of seeds with your little ones. Young minds will sprout new knowledge about the importance of seeds in their world.

*ideas contributed by Diane Gilliam and Angie Kutzer*

### Seed Start-Up

Gather several different kinds of seeds and put each kind into a separate container. To begin the seed study, pass the containers around the group and direct your little ones to inspect each variety. Discuss the similarities and differences among the seeds. Emphasize that—while the varieties may look different—they are all *seeds*. Then give your youngsters more information by reading the book *All About Seeds* (Now I Know series), by Susan Kuchalla (Troll Associates). Now that the roots of the unit have been established, "grow" on with the next activities!

### Take A Closer Look

Discovering seed parts is easy with this activity. To prepare, soak a bag of dried lima beans in water overnight and duplicate the seed diagram on page 12 for each child. Also enlarge a copy of page 12 for demonstration purposes.

Explain to your little ones that all seeds have three parts in common: the *embryo,* the *food-storage tissue,* and the *seed coat.* Give each child a lima bean and a seed diagram. Point to the seed coat on your enlarged diagram. Inform your children that the seed coat protects the inside of the seed from injury, insects, and loss of water. Instruct each student to color the seed coat on her diagram purple; then have her carefully remove the seed coat from her bean. Next point to the embryo on your diagram. Tell your children that the embryo is the part of the seed that is the baby plant. Instruct each child to color the embryo on her diagram green; then have her open her seed and find the embryo. Point to the food-storage tissue on your diagram. Explain that the food-storage tissue contains all the food needed for the baby plant to begin to grow. Instruct each student to color the food-storage tissue on her diagram yellow; then have her find the tissue in her bean. This dissection activity is sure to make your little ones more "part-smart" about seeds!

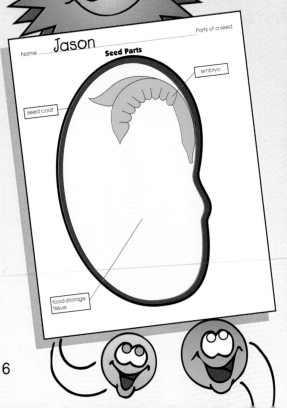

Name _Jason_   Parts of a seed
**Seed Parts**
embryo
seed coat
food-storage tissue

## Down And Dirty

Now your youngsters are ready to dig into the dirt and plant their own seeds. You will need to round up a bag of potting soil, individual containers, some seeds (bean seeds sprout quickly), and misting bottles. Set up this planting station in your sand table or outside for easy cleanup. Duplicate, color, and cut apart the cards on page 13 to use in a pocket chart.

Before the planting begins, share the book *Bean And Plant* (Stopwatch Books series), by Christine Back and Barrie Watts (Silver Burdett Company). This book gives an up close, pictorial account of the growth process of a seed. After reading the book, display the planting cards sequentially in a pocket chart. Explain the necessary steps in planting a seed. Leave the cards in the chart for future reference. Invite each child to plant her own seed using the materials provided. You will also need to plant five extra seeds for the experiments in the "Seed Needs" activity on page 8. Dig in!

## A Planter's Guide

Invite your new planting pros to assemble their own how-to booklets. For each child, duplicate a set of cards from page 13 and cut seven flowerpot shapes, about seven inches high, from construction paper. Write the title "How To Plant A Seed" on one pot cutout for each child. Distribute the pot cutouts and the card sets to your children. Direct each child to cut the cards apart and glue a card onto each pot cutout. Explain that the cover should go at the beginning of the book; then have him sequence his pot pages behind it. Once they're in order, staple the booklets together on the left side and encourage your children to use their booklets to teach their families how to plant like a pro!

## Recording Growth

Learning how to observe, measure, and record data are valuable science skills. Give your little ones an opportunity to practice these skills with this journaling activity. To prepare, duplicate enough copies of the journal sheet on page 15 so that each child has four sheets. Store these sheets in a plastic flowerpot. Fill another pot with linking cubes. Place both pots near the sprouting plants from the "Down And Dirty" activity. Periodically invite each student to go over and complete a journal sheet by drawing a picture of his plant; making a rod of cubes equal to his plant's height; coloring the same number of cubes on the journal sheet; and signing his name. Date and save the sheets for each child. When four observations have been made, urge him to take his journal and his plant home to enjoy.

## Seed Needs

Discuss with your students that just as people need food, clothing, and shelter in order to grow and survive, seeds need three essential things also—sun (or light), water, and soil—in order to grow into healthy plants. Then explore the needs of seeds by setting up these fun experiments.

**A Seed Needs Light:** Use three of the planted seeds from the extras you planted during "Down And Dirty" on page 7 to show that seeds need light in order to grow into healthy plants. Place one container in a closet or cabinet so that it receives no light. Cut a small hole toward the bottom of a paper bag and invert the bag over another container so that it receives only a little light. Place the third container in full sunlight. Have students water all the seeds as needed and check periodically for any changes. In a week or so, the seed in sunlight should have grown into a healthy, green plant; the seed in the bag should have grown into a limp, yellowish plant; and the seed in the closet will have only grown a little, if any.

**A Seed Needs Water:** Once the other two extra seeds you planted have grown into small plants, use them to show that seeds need water in order to grow. Label the containers as shown. Have a child water the designated plant daily. Direct the whole class to take a daily peek to see what is happening.

## Stylish Seeds

Encourage your little ones to make a fashion statement with these seed pendants. Provide simple shape patterns, tagboard, glue, yarn, hole punchers, scissors, and an assortment of dried beans and seeds. To make a necklace, have each child choose a shape pattern to trace and cut from tagboard; then punch a hole in his shape cutout. Direct the child to apply a layer of glue to the cutout and cover it with seeds and beans—being careful not to cover up the hole. Challenge more advanced students to make patterns or designs on their cutouts. When the glue has dried, help the child cut a length of yarn and thread it through the hole. Assist him with tying the yarn's ends together. These snazzy pendants will be the rage of the room!

**Pam Crane**

## Seed Safari

Sprinkle your young sprouts with a little more knowledge about seeds by discussing how seeds travel. On the chalkboard, list all volunteered answers to the question, "How do seeds get around?" Then have your children evaluate their answers after you read *Seeds Get Around* by Nancy White, published by Newbridge Communications, Inc. (This book can be ordered from Newbridge at 1-800-867-0307.)

## Traveling Seeds Song

Once your little ones are versed on seed travel, teach them the following song to enhance their understanding.

*(sung to the tune of "London Bridge")*

See the small seeds falling down,
Falling down, falling down.
See the small seeds falling down,
Grow, seeds, grow.

See the winged seeds in the wind,
In the wind, in the wind.
See the winged seeds in the wind,
Fly, seeds, fly.

See the big seeds in the sea,
In the sea, in the sea.
See the big seeds in the sea,
Float, seeds, float.

See the hooked seeds on my socks,
On my socks, on my socks.
See the hooked seeds on my socks,
Ride, seeds, ride.

## Breezy, The Flying Seed

A draft of laughter will gust through the classroom after your little ones make their own Breezy, a twirling winged seed. For each child, duplicate the pattern on page 15 on construction paper. Have each child cut out her pattern. Assist her in using the dotted lines as a guide to fold one wing forward and the other wing backward. Show her how to attach a paper clip to the bottom of Breezy. Hold Breezy up as high as possible; then let go and watch the seed go swirling and twirling to the ground. After some free exploration time, encourage your students to use Breezy at home to explain to their families one way that seeds travel.

## The Green-Bean Scene

Green beans will help your little ones "suc-seed" in this counting and comparing activity. To prepare, you will need a bag of fresh green beans (peas still in the pod can be a substitution) and a bag of jelly beans. Seat a small group of children in a circle around the bag of green beans. Instruct each child to choose a bean pod from the bag and open it. Have him count the seeds in his pod. When everyone has counted, ask "Who has the most (fewest, same amount of) seeds?" The child with the most gets a jelly bean. In case of a tie, both children get jelly beans. Continue until all children in the group have jelly beans to eat.

## Estimation Situation

Gather several seedy fruits—such as an apple, a pear, a peach, a plum, and an orange—a marker, and chart paper and set up this estimation situation. Draw a simple, enlarged outline of each fruit on the chart paper. Also draw a box in the middle of each outline. Hold up one fruit and ask your children to estimate the number of seeds it contains. List volunteers' initials and estimations inside the fruit outline. Then cut the fruit open and dislodge the seeds. Count the seeds together. Go back through the listed estimates and circle any correct guesses. Record the actual number of seeds inside the box. All of that estimating will make a youngster hungry, so be sure to share the fruits of their labor!

## Show Me Your Seeds!

Germinate some parent involvement and create an informative display with this activity. Duplicate a parent note and a seed card from page 14 for each child. Prepare a bulletin-board background with the seed essentials—sun, soil, and water—and title the display "Look At Our Seeds!" As students bring in their seed collections, invite each child to show her favorite seed to the class. Glue or tape this seed to a seed card and label it. Pin the card to the soil section of the bulletin board. Your youngsters will enjoy seeing the class collection grow!

## Books To Grow On

Celebrate seeds with a special seed snack of nuts, granola, or trail mix and a good seed story from the list below.

*The Tiny Seed*
Written by Eric Carle
Published by Simon & Schuster, Inc.

*The Carrot Seed*
Written by Ruth Krauss
Published by HarperCollins Children's Books

*Flowers • Fruits • Seeds*
Written by Jerome Wexler
Published by Simon & Schuster, Inc.

*Backyard Sunflower*
Written and Photographed by Elizabeth King
Published by Dutton Children's Books

## Seed Shakers

Let your little ones shake, rattle, and roll using these fun instruments. Provide cups, pie pans, paper plates, stickers, markers, masking tape, and an assortment of seeds. Instruct each child to make a shaker by choosing a container and filling it with seeds. Seal each child's shaker by inverting another cup, plate, or pan and securing it with masking tape. Invite each child to decorate his shaker with stickers and markers. Have the children use their shakers to add a little rhythm to the song below. Once it has been perfected, perform the song for another class or for parents.

## We Need Seeds

*(sung to the tune of "The Muffin Man")*

Oh, do you know that seeds need soil,
Seeds need soil, seeds need soil?
Oh, do you know that seeds need soil,
To grow and grow and grow?

Oh, do you know that seeds need rain…

Oh, do you know that seeds need sun…

Oh, do you know that we need seeds…

# Seed Parts

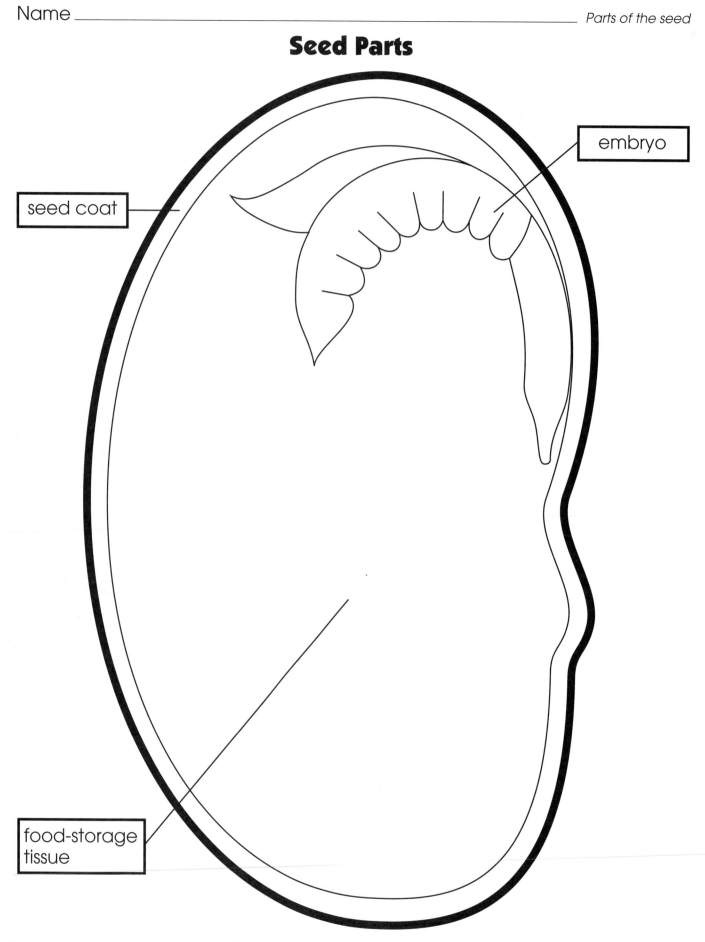

embryo

seed coat

food-storage tissue

**Note To The Teacher:** Use this diagram with "Take A Closer Look" on page 6.

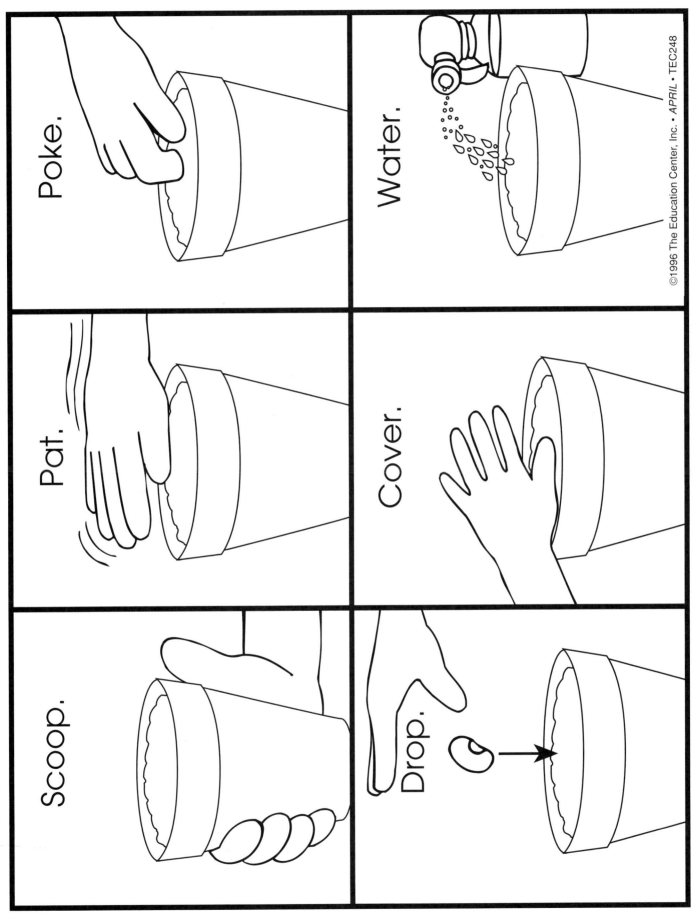

Poke.

Water.

Pat.

Cover.

Scoop.

Drop.

©1996 The Education Center, Inc. • *APRIL* • TEC248

## Parent Note

Use with "Show Me Your Seeds!" on page 10.

Dear Family,
    We are exploring the magical world of seeds and need your assistance. Would you please help me fill an empty egg carton with 12 different types of seeds? (Dried beans and nuts are seeds, too!) I will also need you to label each egg cup with the seed name. Please remind me to carry my seed collection to school on _____. Thanks for your excitement over seeds! I can't wait to show my friends!

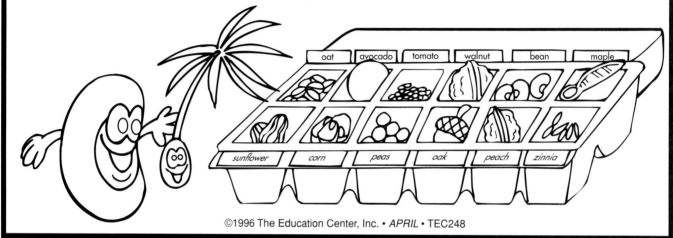

## Seed Display Card

Use with "Show Me Your Seeds!" on page 10.

_____'s

favorite seed:

## Breezy Pattern

Use with "Breezy, The Flying Seed" on page 9.

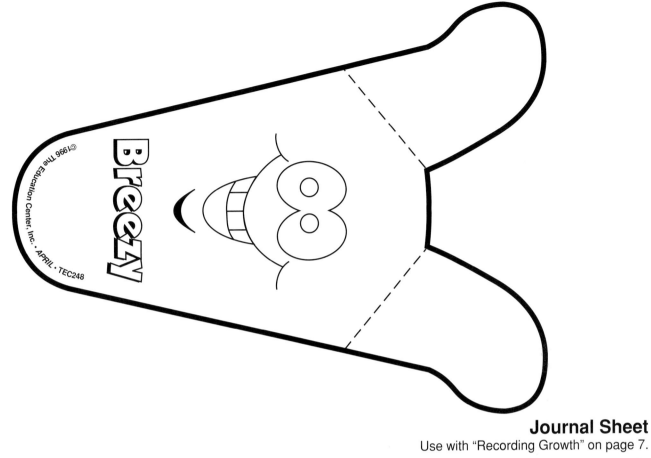

## Journal Sheet

Use with "Recording Growth" on page 7.

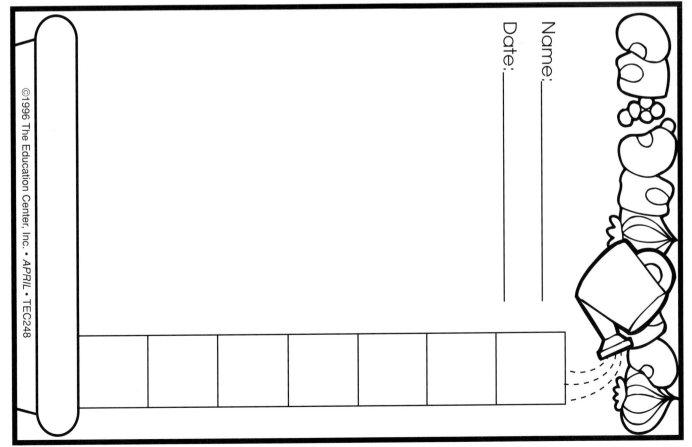

# April Showers

April showers bring...exciting learning opportunities! Come rain or shine, your youngsters are sure to enjoy these radical rain activities.

ideas contributed by Vicki Pacchetti

### Rainstorm Brainstorm

Pop open an umbrella and let the shower of ideas begin! To prepare for this brainstorming activity, cut at least one construction-paper raindrop shape for every child. Punch a hole in each raindrop and tie on a length of clear fishing line. On a rainy day, gather your little ones near a window to briefly observe the rain and its effects. Or ask each child to close his eyes as you play a recording of a rainstorm (available from nature stores). Ask your young "meteorologists" to share an observation of rain or an experience they have had with rain. Write each child's thought on a raindrop. Tie each child's raindrop to the spokes of the open umbrella; then suspend the umbrella from your ceiling. As the class learns more about rain and the water cycle, have them suggest thoughts to record on additional raindrops. It's raining! It's pouring!

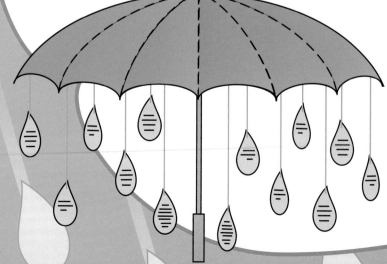

### Rainy-Day Adventure

Rainy days provide the perfect opportunity to learn about cause and effect. As you begin your study of rain, ask parents to send extra umbrellas to your classroom for use during your unit. When the weather is expected to provide gentle showers—and thunder and lightning are unlikely—provide each child with an umbrella and go outdoors. Ask youngsters to observe the sights and sounds of the rain. If desired, take along an instant camera to record your group's adventures. When you return to your classroom, have students help you write a description of the experience along with the group's discoveries. Display this story along with the photos or with students' drawings of your rainy-day adventure.

## Wet Weather

The forecast for this weather-charting activity calls for rain with a good chance of learning. For older learners, duplicate a class supply plus one extra of the weather chart and stickers on page 22; then program the extra chart so that the dates in the squares correspond to the days of your unit. Ask each child to refer to this example to complete his own chart. For younger learners, duplicate a classroom supply of a programmed chart and the sticker set. Cut or have the children cut the chart and the set of stickers along the bold lines. Encourage each child to color his stickers.

Next make a class supply of sticker-making solution by mixing together one cup of hot water, two envelopes of unflavored gelatin, and one-half teaspoon of peppermint extract (optional). When this mixture has cooled, have each child use a cotton ball to spread it over the back of his set of stickers. When the stickers have dried, cut each set apart on the dotted lines and store the sets in personalized resealable bags.

Explain the "rain" and "no rain" symbols. Each day of your unit, ask each child to record the weather by licking and sticking the appropriate sticker to his chart. This is one activity your little ones are sure to stick with!

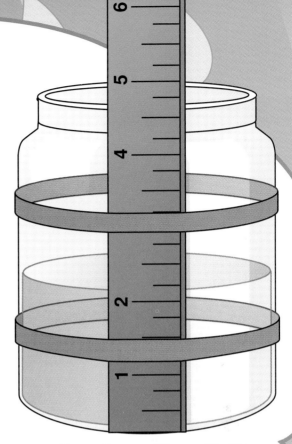

## Raindrops Keep Falling

If raindrops just keep falling and falling, take a moment to prepare an informal rain gauge to get an idea of the rainfall amount your area is getting. Remove the label from a clean peanut-butter jar. Using rubberbands, attach a plastic ruler to the outside of the jar. Place the rain gauge in an area outdoors where it will remain undisturbed. As you check the jar daily, younger learners will be fascinated by the increase in the amount of rain collected. Help older learners record on a graph the amount of rain collected. Pretty soon everyone will be in anticipation of precipitation!

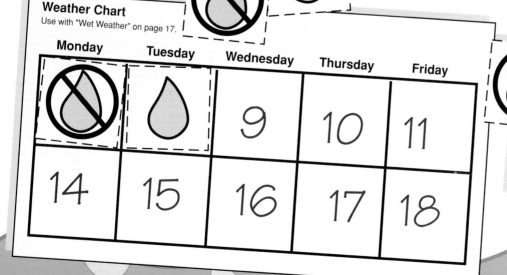

**Weather Chart**
Use with "Wet Weather" on page 17.

| Monday | Tuesday | Wednesday | Thursday | Friday |
|--------|---------|-----------|----------|--------|
|        |         | 9 | 10 | 11 |
| 14 | 15 | 16 | 17 | 18 |

# Where Does Rain Come From?

Answer curious youngsters' questions about rain and explain the water cycle using the full-color flannelboard pieces on page 23. First duplicate the umbrella patterns on page 24 for future use before cutting out the flannelboard pieces. Mount the pieces on tagboard; then laminate them for durability. Back each piece with self-adhesive felt. Use these flannelboard pieces to accompany the following poem and to enhance "The Water-Cycle Chant."

## The Adventures Of Randy The Raindrop

Randy the *raindrop* lived in a *cloud*.
The heat from the sun made him big, strong, and proud!
He grew heavy and big 'til one day—oh my!
He fell right through the floor of his house in the sky!

He was scared; then he noticed some more raindrops falling.
"Hey, Randy, isn't this fun?" they were calling.
Then onto a leaf, with a splash Randy fell.
And what happened next is a strange thing to tell.

Randy was made of water, you know.
And part of him went to help the tree grow.
The rest of him sat in a puddle so round;
Then the sun came out and shone on the ground.

The sun warmed Randy and he started to change.
He became *water vapor*—my that felt strange!
Little drops of vapor—too tiny to see—
Floated into the sky. Yes, that was Randy!

Randy's home once again was a *cloud* in the sky.
He was a *raindrop* once more. But then, by and by...
The sun made him bigger, and bigger, and then—
He fell through the floor of his house once again!

## The Water-Cycle Chant

*(chanted to the rhythm of
"Peanut, Peanut Butter")*

**Chorus:**
Water, water cycle—*(whisper)* that's rain!
Water, water cycle—*(whisper)* that's rain!

**Verses:**
First there is a cloud and it rains. It rains.
It really, really rains.
*"Rain" fingers downward.*

Rain fills up the oceans, the oceans.
It really fills the oceans.
*Make larger and larger circles with both hands.*

The sun comes out and shines. It shines.
It really, really shines.
*Form a circle overhead with arms.*

The water vapor floats up. It floats up.
It really, really floats up.
*Point to the sky.*

The water vapor forms a cloud, a cloud.
It really forms a cloud.
*Clasp hands together.*

And once again it rains. It rains.
It really, really rains.
*"Rain" fingers downward.*

## Umbrella Bridges

Don't let the weather rain on your parade! Use this movement activity to add some zip to rainy days. For safety reasons, cover the ends of the spokes of an umbrella with masking tape. Ask two student volunteers to face each other and hold opposite sides of the umbrella over their heads. As the class sings the following song, direct students to parade around the room and under the umbrella. When the group sings, "Here's your umbrella!", the two children holding the umbrella slowly bring it down to "capture" the child under it. The captured child then trades places with one of the children holding the umbrella. No more rainy-day blues!

### Here's Your Umbrella!
*(sung to the tune of "London Bridges")*

The rain outside is falling down, falling down,
  falling down.
The rain outside is falling down.
Here's your umbrella!

## Umbrella Math

Add a splash to math with these umbrella activities. Use the patterns on page 24 to prepare a supply of different-colored, construction-paper or wallpaper umbrella shapes. Then watch as a multitude of math activities pour out of these umbrellas!

- Invite students to work with classmates to put the umbrellas in order by size.
- Encourage youngsters to sort the umbrellas by size, color, or design.
- Divide the umbrellas into unnamed categories. Ask students to find the similarities and differences in the groups.
- Arrange umbrellas to create a pattern. Challenge students to discover and extend the pattern.

## Painting With Rain

A drizzling rain is just what you'll need for this painting project. For each child, cut a paper plate to resemble an umbrella. Ask each child to write his name on the back of the plate; then have him sprinkle powdered tempera paint on the other side of the plate. Have each child either stand outdoors with his shape or hold it out of a window so that it can be sprinkled by the rain. When each child is pleased with his rain-swirled design, have him set it aside to dry. As a finishing touch, have him cut and glue a handle to the dry umbrella. Let the glue dry; then hang students' completed projects from your ceiling or display them on a bulletin board to create a colorful collection of rain-made umbrellas (see "Rainy-Day Blues" on page 20).

### Rainy-Day Blues

Feeling under the weather? Preparing this display will give you a chance to talk with your little ones about the different ways that rain can make people feel. In advance duplicate a pair of raindrops (page 25) onto light blue construction paper for each child. Cut out each pair of raindrops. During a group time, ask youngsters to suggest reasons that rainy weather might make them sad and reasons it might make them happy. Then ask each child to give you reasons for you to write on his raindrops. Display the raindrops on a splatter-painted or foil-wrapping-paper background along with a title. If desired, arrange the students' painted umbrellas (see "Painting With Rain" on page 19) as a colorful border around your display.

*I get to wear my plastic, yellow boots*
*Kari*

*I can't swing when it rains.*
*Kari*

### Wet Wiggle Worms

During stormy days, water fills the tunnels of earthworms' underground homes. Explain to your class that worms have to crawl above ground when rain comes tumbling down. Give each child a pipe cleaner to wind around her index finger. Then invite youngsters to wiggle their worms while singing this squirmy song.

### Little Wiggle Worm
*(sung to the tune of "The Eensy-Weensy Spider")*

| | |
|---|---|
| The little wiggle worm | *Wiggle pipe-cleaner worm.* |
| Went crawling underground. | *Wiggle worm under hand.* |
| Down came the rain; | *Wiggle fingers downward.* |
| Soon mud was all around. | *Make a disgusted face; open arms wide.* |
| | |
| Rain filled the tunnels | *Open hand; move fingers together.* |
| And pushed out little worm. | *Push worm through other hand.* |
| So the puddles on the ground | *Make an O with hand.* |
| Were the only place to squirm. | *Wiggle worm into O.* |

*cluck cluck*

## Puddle Jumping

Youngsters are sure to laugh aloud as you read aloud *The Rain Puddle* by Adelaide Holl (Lothrop, Lee & Shepard Books), a humorous story about farm animals that see their reflections in a puddle. After reading the story, splash into dramatic fun with this idea. Scallop the edges of an extra-long length of aluminum foil to resemble a puddle. Place the puddle on the floor; then have each child decide which farm animal named in the story she would like to portray. Read the story aloud again as youngsters pretend to be the confused animals encountering their reflections.

## Do A Rain Dance!

What to do if you'd like more rainy weather? Why, perform a rain dance, of course! For inspiration, read aloud *April Showers* by George Shannon (Greenwillow Books). As you read, encourage your children to take part in the garden frogs' rain dance. Or follow up the story by playing some lively instrumental music and inviting each child, in turn, to lead the class in a rainy-day romp around your room.

### Stormy Songs

"Puddles"
Sung by Charlotte Diamond
*My Bear Gruff*
Hug Bug Records

"Ducks Like Rain"
Sung by Raffi
*Rise And Shine*
Troubadour Records Ltd.

"It Ain't Gonna' Rain"
/ "Rain, Rain, Go Away"
Sung by Greg & Steve
*Playing Favorites*
Youngheart Records

## More Rainy-Day Literature

Don't save these books for a rainy day. Check them out right away!

*Rain Talk*
Written by Mary Serfozo
Published by Simon & Schuster Children's Books

*It's Raining, It's Pouring*
Written by Kin Eagle
Published by Whispering Coyote Press, Inc.

*Bumpa Rumpus And The Rainy Day*
Written by Joanne Reay
Published by Houghton Mifflin Company

# Weather Chart

Use with "Wet Weather" on page 17.

| Monday | Tuesday | Wednesday | Thursday | Friday |
|--------|---------|-----------|----------|--------|
|        |         |           |          |        |
|        |         |           |          |        |

# Weather Stickers

Use with "Wet Weather" on page 17.

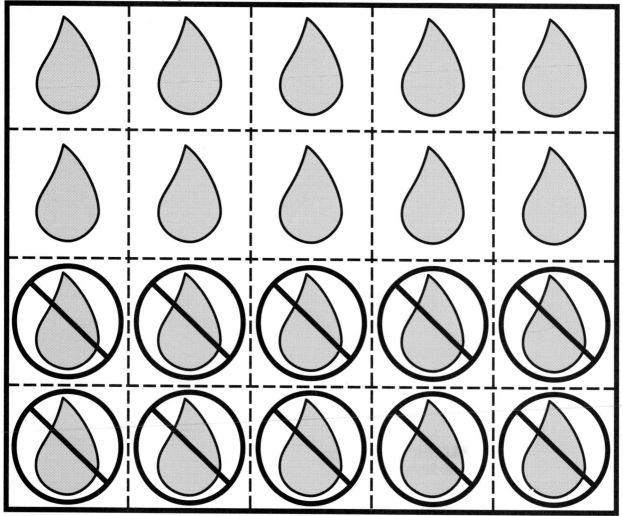

Use with "The Adventures Of Randy The Raindrop" and "The Water-Cycle Chant" on page 18.

**Randy the raindrop**

sun

cloud

water vapor

tree

puddle

# Umbrella Patterns
Use with "Umbrella Math" on page 19.

**Raindrop Patterns**
Use with "Rainy-Day Blues" on page 20.

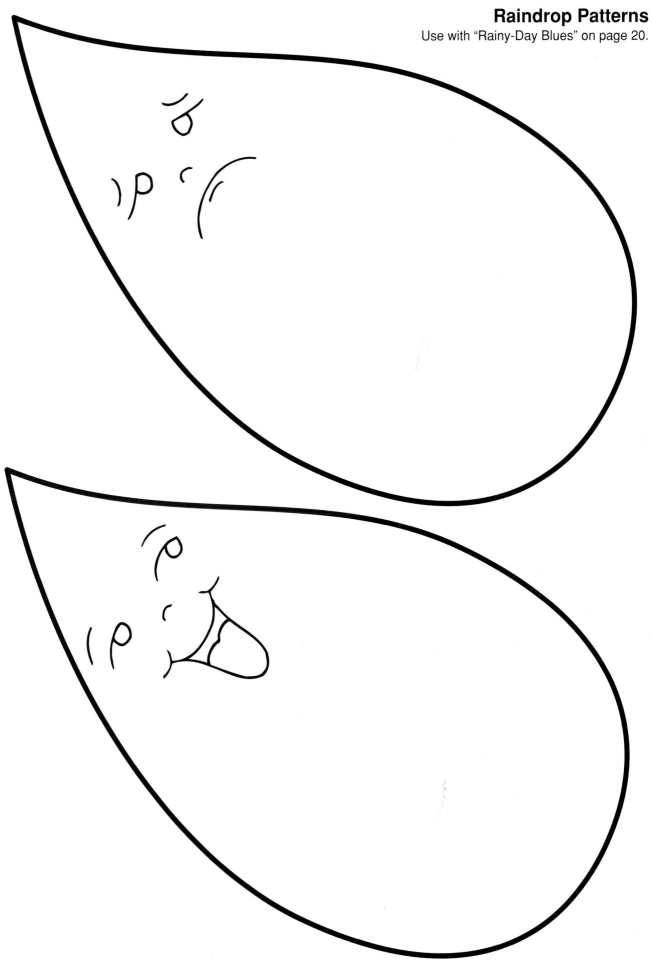

# "Hares" To Bunnies!

Give a cheer because "every-bunny" loves bunnies! And what a perfect time to hop into a unit about rabbits with spring thriving and Easter arriving. So let Peter Cottontail guide you down the trail to lots of exciting bunny-related activities.

*ideas contributed by Jan Brennan and Stacie Davis*

## This Little Bunny

Bound into your bunny unit with this rhyme and the cute bunny pattern on page 30. In advance enlarge the bunny pattern onto chart paper or poster board. Color it as desired; then use masking tape to attach the poster to your chalkboard. Next read the "This Little Bunny" poem below aloud to students. As you read the poem, point out the bunny's features on the poster. Afterward invite students to share what they know about rabbits. Write students' responses on the bunny poster; then hang it in a prominent classroom location.

Bunnies eat carrots.
Charles

They're soft.
Frankie

Bunnies are cute.
Dana

## This Little Bunny

This little bunny has two big ears,
Long and tall to help him hear.
This little bunny has a nose so small,
It helps him smell—but that's not all.
This little bunny has strong legs to hop,
He runs and runs and doesn't like to stop.
This little bunny has short legs in front,
To help him balance when he's on a hunt.
And this little bunny has a fluffy round tail.
It's the last part we see when he hops down the trail.

—Jan Brennan

# A Bonanza Of Bunny Facts

After students have had the opportunity to share their knowledge about bunnies, read aloud a nonfiction book such as *See How They Grow: Rabbit* photographed by Barrie Watts (Lodestar Books). Then share some more fascinating facts about rabbits with your little learners.

- Rabbits rely on their long, sensitive ears to help them hear sounds from all directions.
- Rabbits lose body heat through their ears. This helps keep them cool in hot weather.
- Rabbits have a very keen sense of smell that helps them sense when danger is near.
- Rabbits have very powerful back legs. If frightened, rabbits can leap ten or more feet to escape danger.
- Rabbits will run in a zigzag pattern to escape from enemies.
- Enemies of rabbits include coyotes, foxes, weasels, snakes, hawks, and owls.
- During the summer months, rabbits eat clover, weeds, and grass. During the winter months, rabbits eat twigs, fruit, and bark from bushes and trees.

# Bunches Of Bunnies

Another interesting fact about bunnies—they have lots of babies! To emphasize this fact, share the story *Bunches And Bunches Of Bunnies* by Louise Mathews (Scholastic Inc.). After reading the story, explain that female rabbits reproduce several times a year. Each time rabbits give birth, they have approximately five babies.

Then try this activity to help students better understand this phenomenon. Use two stuffed rabbits to represent the mother and father bunnies and 25 cotton balls to represent baby rabbits. Then enlist students' help in selecting five different calendar dates. (For younger students, ask volunteers to point to five date squares on a yearlong calendar to determine the dates.) Designate those dates as the days on which baby rabbits will be "born." Next ask students to pretend that it is the first date they've selected and put five cotton balls next to the stuffed rabbits. If desired, sing "Happy Birthday To You" to the baby rabbits. Repeat this process four more times. Then enlist students' help in counting how many babies are born to one set of rabbits in a given year. My goodness—that's a lot of brothers and sisters!

## Nibble, Nibble, Crunch!

Tell students that during the winter months—when grass and leaves are scarce or covered with snow—rabbits feed on twigs and bark. During the spring and summer months, rabbits feed on leafy green plants like clover, grass, and weeds. Rabbits also like to nibble on bean sprouts, peas, lettuce, and other vegetables.

Does all this talk of food have your little ones ready for a snack? If so, try making Rabbit-Food Salad. To make the salad, put bite-size lettuce and spinach pieces into a large bowl. (Introduce your students to different varieties of lettuce by using romaine, endive, and/or escarole in the salad.) Mix peas, bean sprouts, and sliced carrots with the greens and you've got yourself a tasty treat that any rabbit would envy! Provide a variety of dressings and give each child a serving of the salad in a disposable bowl. As each child samples his salad, read aloud *The Tale Of Peter Rabbit* by Beatrix Potter (Scholastic Inc.)

## Bunny Tag

After reading aloud *The Tale Of Peter Rabbit*, discuss how Peter's desire for food from Mr. McGregor's garden led to all sorts of problems. Peter had to use speed to escape from the angry Mr. McGregor. Remind students that real rabbits use not only speed but also a zigzag running pattern to escape from their enemies.

With that fact in mind, head outdoors or to the gym to play a game of Bunny Tag. First select one volunteer to be Mr. McGregor. Have the remainder of the students pretend to be rabbits. Designate one area to serve as the rabbits' burrow. Tell each rabbit to find a spot away from the burrow and stand there quietly. Then, on a signal, have Mr. McGregor run toward the rabbits. If a rabbit feels that Mr. McGregor is too close, encourage him to jump forward, then zigzag back and forth as he runs toward safety in the designated burrow. If Mr. McGregor is able to tag a rabbit, the rabbit may be Mr. McGregor for the next round of play. Continue until your little bunnies are ready to flop!

## Bunny Headbands

Get your little ones hopping with these bunny headbands. Provide each child with the following materials: one 2" x 24" strip of white construction paper, one 1" x 4 1/2" strip of white construction paper, two rabbit-ear shapes cut from white construction paper, one rabbit-nose shape cut from pink construction paper, a pink crayon, and glue. To make a headband, first fit each child's 2" x 24" paper strip to his head and staple the ends together. Have him use a pink crayon to color the ears as shown, then glue the ears to his headband. Next direct each student to glue his 1" x 4 1/2" paper strip to the headband as shown. Complete the project by having each child glue the construction-paper nose to the end of the construction-paper strip.

## Bunny Melodies

Teach your students these tunes. Encourage students to wear their headbands while singing and acting out these songs.

### I'm A Little Bunny
*(sung to the tune of "I'm A Little Teapot")*

I'm a little bunny, soft and sweet.
Here are my ears and here are my feet.
When I'm in the garden, I look for treats,
And nibble on all I like to eat.

### My Bunny Hops
### All Through The Garden
*(sung to the tune of "My Bonnie Lies Over The Ocean")*

My bunny hops all through the garden.
My bunny hops all through the yard.
I like to play tag with my bunny,
But trying to catch him is hard.

Come back, come back,
Oh, come back, my bunny, to me, to me.
Come back, come back,
Oh, come back, my bunny, to me.

My bunny is so soft and spunky.
My bunny is a friend to me.
My bunny is such fun to play with.
Come join us and you, too, will see.

Come back, come back,
Oh, come back, my bunny, to me, to me.
Come back, come back,
Oh, come back, my bunny, to me.

### More Bunny Books To Nibble On

Here are some more good books about bunnies, just right for the Easter season—or anytime!

*The April Rabbits* by David Cleveland (Scholastic Inc.)
*The Big Bunny And The Easter Eggs* by Steven Kroll (Scholastic Inc.)
*Bunny Trouble* by Hans Wilhelm (Scholastic Inc.)
*The Little Rabbit Who Wanted Red Wings* by Carolyn Sherwin Bailey (Platt & Munk, Publishers)
*The Big Bunny And The Magic Show* by Steven Kroll (Scholastic Inc.)
*Seven Little Rabbits* by John Becker (Scholastic Inc.)

Come back, come back.
Come back my bunny
to me, to me.

29

# Bunny Pattern
Use with "This Little Bunny" on page 26.

# BILLIONS OF BUBBLES

Give a child a bottle of bubble solution and he'll go wild with excitement! So, why all the commotion over this slippery potion? Could it be the learning opportunities bubbling out of every bubble bottle? Or the practical skills promoted by puffing and popping bubbles? Or just the prospect of pure and simple fun? To find out, make up a batch of this magical mix and let the discovery begin with these activities! Oh, and remember to take lots of pictures of youngsters enjoying this "pop-ular" concoction.

*by Mackie Rhodes*

## BUBBLE BASICS

This basic bubble solution and some simple bubble blowers will have youngsters engaged in a full-blown bubble-blowing blitz in no time at all! Have each child mix a personalized portion of the solution in a lidded container. Or multiply the soap and water amounts to create enough solution to fill containers of different sizes. Then invite students to bubble away using some of the suggested blowers created from simple and inexpensive materials. Also encourage them to explore with other objects to determine which can be used to produce bubbles.

**Simple Solution**
(makes about four ounces)

2 Tbsp. dishwashing liquid
1/2 cup water

**Super-Sized Solution**
(makes about one gallon)

1 3/4 cups dishwashing liquid
14 cups water

## BODACIOUS BLOWERS

- Cut out the center of a margarine-tub lid. Dip the flat side of the resulting ring into a flat container of the bubble solution; then gently blow the soap film into a bubble.
- Cut off the top third of a plastic soda bottle (any size). If desired, edge the wide end of the blower with vinyl tape. Dip the narrow end into the bubble solution; then blow through the wide end of the blower.
- Cut off the bottom of the remainder of the soda bottle. If desired, edge one end of the resulting tube with vinyl tape. Dip the unfinished end of the tube into the bubble solution; then gently blow through the taped end of the tube.
- Dip one end of a piece of rigatoni or wagon-wheel pasta into the bubble solution; then blow through the other end.
- Dip the frames of a pair of sunglasses (without the lenses) into the bubble solution; then gently blow each side to create double bubbles!
- Dip a cookie cutter into the bubble solution; then gently blow the resulting soap film.

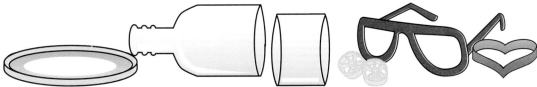

## BUBBLE SOLUTION CONFUSION

With the wide assortment of liquid soaps available, how do you know which is best for bubble solution? Try this experiment with your students to clear up the confusion. Partially fill each of several different containers with 1/2 cup of water. Label each container with a different kind of liquid soap—such as bubble bath, hand soap, laundry detergent, dishwashing liquid, or baby shampoo; then mix 1/8 cup of each soap into its corresponding container. Invite youngsters to blow bubbles with each of the different solutions. Which of the solutions create bubbles? Which do not? Record the findings on a bulletin-board paper cutout of a bubble bottle programmed with two columns—one labeled "Yes" and the other "No." Then have students blow bubbles from the solutions listed in the "Yes" column. Is one solution better than all the others for bubble blowing? Invite youngsters to mix up a personalized amount of their favorite bubble solution to take home.

## BUBBLE PENS

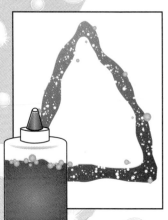

These bubble pens will have little ones bursting with enthusiasm for writing! To make a bubble pen, mix a tablespoon of dry tempera paint with the simple solution for bubbles provided in "Bubble Basics" on page 31. Pour a small amount of the colored solution into an empty, clean glue bottle. Put the lid securely on the bottle, making sure the tip is completely closed. Have a child shake the bottle vigorously to create bubbles inside. Help him open the bottle tip *slightly* so that a steady stream of bubbles flows from the bottle when he squeezes it. Encourage the child to draw shapes, designs, or letters on a sheet of finger-paint paper. Have him close the bottle tip before shaking the bottle to create more bubbles. Replenish the bubble solution in the bottle as necessary. After the bubbles dry, invite youngsters to take their bubble writings home to share with their families.

## CAREFREE CRUISING

Teach youngsters this finger rhyme for some bouncy, bubbly fun.

| | |
|---|---|
| Five little bubbles cruising through the air. | *Hold up five fingers. Close fist.* |
| The first bubble said, "I haven't a care!" | *Hold up index finger.* |
| The second bubble said, "It's warm in the sun." | *Hold up middle finger.* |
| The third bubble said, "I'm having such fun!" | *Hold up ring finger.* |
| The fourth bubble said, "It's great to be free." | *Hold up little finger.* |
| The fifth bubble said, "I'm happy as can be!" | *Hold up thumb.* |
| A bird flies by. | *Flap hands.* |
| Its wings go flop. | |
| Five bubbles—Pop! Pop! Pop! Pop! Pop! | *Poke finger into air five times.* |

## RAINBOW BUBBLES

While youngsters are puffing and popping up a bubble wonderland, call their attention to the rainbow of colors on the surfaces of these shimmering spheres. Then, during a small-group activity, invite students to create their own models of a colorful bubble. For each child, cut a circle from a sheet of white tagboard; then cut out the center to create a ring. Glue a slightly larger sheet of waxed paper to each side of the ring. After the glue dries, trim the excess waxed paper from around the ring. Then invite the child to use watercolor markers in a rainbow of colors to decorate her bubble. After she has applied the desired colors on one side of her bubble, have her wipe away the beaded marker drops from the surface so that a colorful opaque appearance results. Then have her repeat the process on the other side of the bubble. Display the bubbles on the background created in "Beautiful Bubbly Bulletin Board."

## BEAUTIFUL BUBBLY BULLETIN BOARD

Put your youngsters' pucker power to work to produce bountiful bubbles for this beautiful bulletin-board background! To prepare, mix several containers of colored bubble solution as described in "Bubble Pens" on page 32. Then spread a length of white bulletin-board paper over a table. Invite small groups of youngsters, in turn, to blow colored bubbles *down* onto the paper. Keep plenty of paper towels on hand to wipe bubble-burst splashes off arms and faces. After the paper is completely covered with bubble prints and splashes, allow the bubble paint to dry. Then hang the decorative background paper on a bulletin board. If desired, edge the board with strips of colored, plastic bubble wrap. Use the board to display the photographs taken during your bubble activities, along with the bubbles made in "Rainbow Bubbles." Title the display "Billions Of Bubbles!"

### BUBBLY BOOKS
*Bubble Bubble*
Written by Mercer Mayer
Published by Rain Bird Productions

*Bubbles, Bubbles, Everywhere*
Written by Melvin Berger and Dwight Kuhn
Published by Newbridge Communications, Inc.
(This book can be ordered from
Newbridge at 1-800-867-0307.)

*The Bubble Factory*
Written by Tomie dePaola
Published by Grosset & Dunlap, Inc.

# BUBBLEFEST!

It's time to celebrate those glorious gliding globes with a festive finale! Use these activities and songs to create the best bubble bash ever!

### BUBBLE FACTORIES

Prepare for your BubbleFest with a variety of bubble-manufacturing centers. Arrange each center—preferably outdoors—so that it contains a bubble solution and tools unique to that center. For instance, you might place cookie-cutter blowers and a baby-shampoo solution in one center, dish-washing-liquid solution and tube blowers in another, and liquid-hand-soap solution and pasta blowers in a third center. Be sure to mix appropriate quantities of water and soap to create solutions that actually create bubbles! For variety, put some bubble-solution ice cubes, a small amount of water, and some plastic bubble wands in the water table. Or partially fill a plastic swimming pool with bubble solution; then provide sieves, colanders, funnels, and a variety of other household items that can be used as bubble-blowing tools. Invite youngsters to participate in a bubble-blowing blizzard as they visit each center!

### "BUBBLE-FLY" CHASE

Delight youngsters with a rambunctious romp of "bubble-fly" chasing. What's a "bubble-fly"? It's a combination of imagination and a bountiful supply of bubbles. Ask a group of volunteers to blow bubbles in a spacious outdoor area. Prompt the other youngsters to imagine the bubbles to be anything that flies—a bird, a butterfly, or even a fly ball! Invite them to use their tools of choice to pop the bubbles—a flyswatter, a butterfly net, or a foam baseball bat. Ready, set, blow! The chase is on!

### HAVE MILK, WILL BUBBLE!

Whole milk, chocolate milk, bubble milk. *Bubble milk?* Of course! It's a traditional childhood favorite! To make bubble milk, stand a resealable plastic sandwich bag upright in a strawberry basket; then pour 1/2 cup of milk into the bag. Poke a small hole in one side of the bag just under the zipper; then force one end of a straw into the hole. Seal the bag tightly. At snacktime, invite each child to blow bubbles into his bag of milk to create bubble milk. As the bag fills with bubbles and air, encourage him to sip some of the milk out to relieve the air pressure, then blow again for more bubble milk. Serve doughnut holes to round out your BubbleFest snack.

# BURST INTO SONG

During your BubbleFest—or any other bubble-blowing occasion—invite youngsters to join you in a few bubbly rounds of some of these songs. Before long, little ones will be popping out their own original tunes!

## BIG AND BOUNCY BUBBLES
*(sung to the tune of "Apples And Bananas")*

I like to blow, blow, blow
Big and bouncy bubbles.
I like to blow, blow, blow
Big and bouncy bubbles.

I like to blow, blow, blow,
Bitsy baby bubbles.
I like to blow, blow, blow,
Bitsy baby bubbles.

I like to pop, pop, pop
Pretty prancing bubbles.
I like to pop, pop, pop
Pretty prancing bubbles.

I like to pop, pop, pop
Piles and piles of bubbles.
I like to pop, pop, pop
Piles and piles of bubbles.

## POP! GO THE BUBBLES
*(sung to the tune of "Pop Goes The Weasel")*

All around the great outdoors
The children chased the bubbles.
The children laughed and had such fun.
Pop! go the bubbles.

## BUBBLES GO 'ROUND THE SUN
*(sung to the tune of "Sally Go 'Round The Sun")*

Bubbles go 'round the sun.
Bubbles go 'round the moon.
Bubbles go 'round the chimney top
All the afternoon. Pop!

## MY BUBBLE
*(sung to the tune of "My Bonnie")*

My bubble floats over the housetop.
My bubble floats over the tree.
My bubble floats over the hilltop.
Oh, come back, my bubble, to me.

Come back, come back;
Oh, come back, my bubble, to me, to me.
Come back, come back;
Oh, come back, my bub....pop! Oh, gee!

# Plunge Into Pond Life!

A *pond* is "a small body of still water," but it is teeming with activity—crickets chirping, frogs leaping, fish swimming, and turtles sunning. Use this across-the-curriculum collection of activities and take the plunge. Make the pond come to life for your little ones!

*ideas contributed by Suzanne Moore and Ada Hanley Goren*

## Peek At A Pond

Introduce the topic of pond life to your youngsters with a frog's-eye peek at life in a small pond. Share *In The Small, Small Pond* by Denise Fleming (Henry Holt & Company, Inc.). After a first read-through, ask students to name animals that use the pond as their home. Encourage students to name animals from the story as well as any others they might know. Record their responses on a sheet of chart paper. Next reread the story, stopping after each animal's action, and invite your students to act out the movements of the pond creatures. Challenge students to act out the movements for the other pond creatures on the list, too. Your classroom will be filled with youngsters swimming like fish, hopping and diving like frogs, crawling and climbing like insects, and slithering like snakes!

Take the plunge...
Share a book with your child!

**Lily Pad Pond**
Written by Bianca Lavies
Published by Dutton Children's Books

**Jump, Frog, Jump!**
Written by Robert Kalan
Published by Greenwillow Books

**Splash!**
Written by Ann Jonas
Published by Greenwillow Books

**Do Not Disturb**
Written by Nancy Tafuri
Published by Greenwillow Books

**In The Pond**
Written by Ermanno Cristini & Luigi Puricelli
Published by Picture Book Studio USA

## Literature To Leap Over

Encourage parents and children to share books about pond life when you send home student-decorated bookmarks. Duplicate the bookmark on page 42 for each child. Have each student color his bookmark and cut it out. Provide each student with a 4 1/2" x 8" piece of construction paper and have him glue his bookmark to it, leaving a small border on all sides. What better way to plunge your students and their parents into visiting the library and reading together!

## Ready To Explore?

Visiting a pond can be a fun-filled and eye-opening experience. If possible, arrange a field trip to a nearby pond for your little ones to explore. (Be sure to ask for several parent volunteers to accompany you on the trip because increased supervision is needed at a pond.)

Prepare your youngsters for this experience by providing each student with an exploration kit. First send home a copy of the parent note on page 42 with each student. When enough materials have been sent in, assemble the following items in a gallon-sized, resealable plastic bag for each student: a small, plastic magnifying glass; a three-ounce clear plastic cup; snack-sized resealable plastic bags (for plant and dirt samples); two craft sticks; and a plastic spoon. Punch two holes at the top of the bag and thread 36 inches of yarn through the holes to make the kit into a necklace. Make a teacher kit for yourself too. Include all of the items in the student kit as well as a colander and a few jars with lids for short-term viewing of aquatic life.

Before departing for the pond, discuss safety precautions with your students—explaining that they should not drink the pond water, should not go into the water, and should be careful at the pond's slippery edge. Encourage students to use the items in their kits to explore the plant life and dirt around the pond, as well as the creatures in the water at the edge of the pond. If a field trip to a pond is not possible, students can use the exploration kits at the classroom pond center described in "Create A Pond." As the students are eagerly exploring the pond or the pond center, take pictures to use for "Sights At The Pond" (page 38). Or, if desired, purchase a disposable camera for your students to share for their own picture taking. No matter who takes the pictures, this hands-on activity will be memorable!

## Create A Pond

If it's not possible to take your youngsters to visit a pond, ponder this idea! Create a pond environment in the classroom with the help of a baby wading pool and a very large rubber tub. The tub will be the pond and the pool will contain the surrounding grass. To make the grassy area, partially fill the pool with Styrofoam® packing peanuts. Set the rubber tub inside the pool, at one edge. Fill the remainder of the pool with Easter grass. If possible obtain pond water to pour into the rubber tub. If pond water is unavailable, place a layer of potting soil in the bottom of the tub; then fill it with water. Create lily pads for the pond by cutting circles of craft foam and then cutting out a slice from each one as shown. Add vinyl or plastic pond critters—such as frogs, snakes, bugs, and turtles—as well as plastic plants. Divide students into small groups to visit the center and use the exploration kits from "Ready To Explore?"

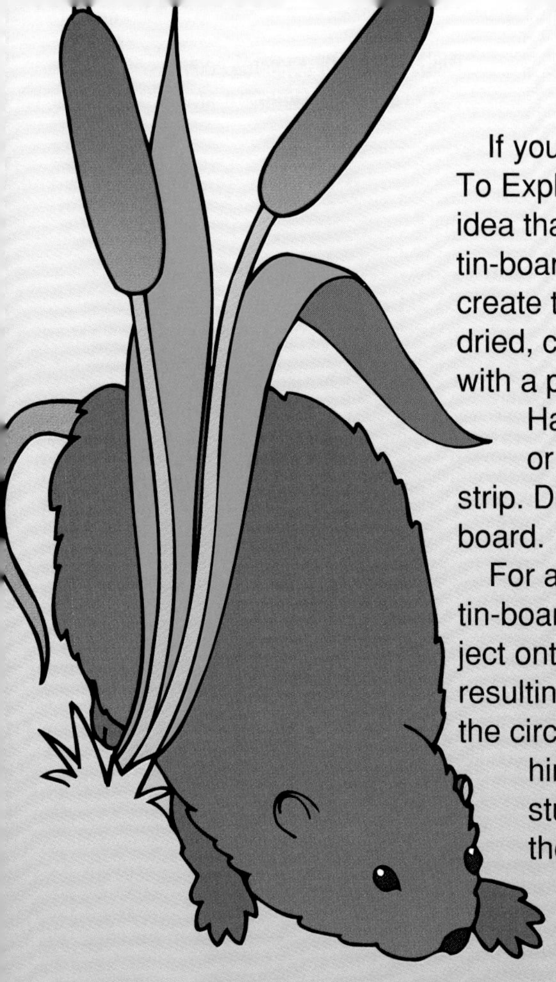

## Sights At The Pond

If you took photos during the field trip or at the pond center (see "Ready To Explore?" on page 37), involve your little ones in this bulletin-board idea that combines art and writing. Begin by cutting a piece of white bulletin-board paper to fit your board. Invite students to use blue finger paint to create the pond water on the bulletin-board paper. After the paint has dried, cover the bulletin board with the paper. Next provide each student with a photograph taken on the field trip to the pond or at the pond center.

Have each student dictate to you something he learned about ponds or pond animals. Record each student's response on a sentence strip. Display the photographs and the sentence strips on the bulletin board.

For a final touch, invite your youngsters to make lily pads for the bulletin-board pond. To make a lily pad, have each student trace a round object onto green construction paper. Show each student how to cut on the resulting outline to make a circle, then how to cut a narrow wedge from the circle. Ask each student to write his name on his lily pad. Next give him a coffee filter that has been folded in half four times. Help each student trim his filter as shown below. Instruct students to unfold their filters and glue them to the green cutouts to resemble water lilies in full bloom. Mount the lilies around the photographs and add the title "Sights At The Pond" for a one-of-a-kind bulletin-board display.

## Lily-Pad Pond Snacks

After making and eating these tasty lily pads, your students will be leaping for more. First photocopy page 44 for later use. After removing page 43 from this book, glue it to a piece of tagboard. Let the glue dry. Laminate the page; then cut apart the cards on the bold lines. Arrange the ingredients and utensils along with the recipe cards at a table. Then invite students to make their own snacks.

### Lily-Pad Pond Snack

**Ingredients For One:**
1 spoonful soft cream cheese
blue food coloring
1/2 English muffin
3 cucumber slices
1 Gummy Frog®

**Utensils:** plastic knife, paper plate

**Teacher Preparation:**
Tint soft cream cheese with blue food coloring.
Peel and slice cucumbers into very thin rounds.
Cut a wedge from each cucumber slice.

# Dive Into These Centers!

Extend the theme of pond life throughout your classroom with these ideas for enhancing some of your learning centers.

**Block Center:** Cut out a pond shape from blue bulletin-board paper and place it on the floor in your block center. Paint lily pads on the paper and add vinyl or stuffed animals, such as turtles, fish, and snakes. Invite your little ones to use blocks to build a dock or a fishing pier. For added excitement provide wooden dowels to serve as fishing poles.

**Art Center:** Challenge your youngsters to make their own pond animals using a variety of materials that float, such as craft foam, meat trays, and Styrofoam® cups and plates. Also place waterproof markers, pipe cleaners, straws, and scissors at the center. Assist students in putting together their animals with hot glue. Then invite students to test-float their critters in the pond center or water table.

**Writing Center:** Provide each student with a pond life journal to record her experiences and observations during your study of pond life. To make the journals, duplicate a journal cover on page 44 for each student. Have each student color her cover; then staple a few blank pieces of paper (cut the same size) behind it. If desired, add a piece of construction paper to the back of each journal for sturdier support. Place both fiction and nonfiction books with pictures at your writing center for students to use as references. Good choices for nonfiction books are *Pond And River* by Steve Parker (Alfred A. Knopf, Inc.) and *Pond Life* by Lynn Stone (Childrens Press). If possible, supply posters of ponds and pond animals, too.

**Math Center:** Use pond objects as math manipulatives for practice with size differentiation. Provide silk plants, craft-foam or construction-paper lily pads, and plastic insects in different sizes. Place them in your math center and encourage your little ones to place the plants in order from smallest to largest, and then repeat the activity with the lily pads and the insects. Students can also count the objects and sort them based on size, shape, or color.

## Have You Seen My...

Share *Have You Seen My Duckling?* by Nancy Tafuri (Mulberry Books) with your little ones. In this picture book, a mother duck leads her ducklings around the pond as she searches for one missing duckling. She stops along the way to ask several pond creatures if they have seen her missing duckling. After sharing the story, have each student draw and cut out a pond animal of her choice. Next divide the class into pairs to play a game that mimics the events in the story. Choose one pair of students to go first. One child closes her eyes while the other child hides her animal cutout in the classroom. The owner then begins to ask her classmates, "Have you seen my [name of pond animal]?" Her classmates may help by giving clues to help locate the animal. When the animal has been found, have the two students switch places so the other partner gets a turn to search. Continue the game until each pair of students has had a turn to play.

## What A Change!

From egg to tadpole to frog, the life cycle of a frog is more than fascinating. Introduce your youngsters to this metamorphosis by reading aloud *Fish Is Fish* by Leo Lionni (Dragonfly Books). After reading the story, duplicate six copies of the life-cycle picture cards on page 45. Color one set of the cards and laminate them for durability, if desired. Share the colored set of cards with your students as you explain the sequence of a frog's life cycle.

Then have your students work together to create life-cycle projects. Divide the class into groups of six students and assign each child in a group a different stage of a frog's life cycle. Cut out the picture cards on the remaining five copies of page 45. Provide each student in a group with the picture card for his assigned stage of the life cycle and a ball of play dough. (Students creating step one will need white dough; all others need green dough.) Invite each student to use his play dough to sculpt a figure in the appropriate stage of the life cycle. When the projects are complete, have students in each group place their creations in sequence to make a display of a frog's life cycle.

# Come Out Of Your Shell

What better way to teach your youngsters about turtles than by having them make one? Begin the lesson by sharing with your students the following facts about turtles:

- Turtles enjoy sunning themselves on logs in ponds.
- Turtles are the only reptiles with shells for protection from their enemies.
- The color of the shell can be black, dark brown, or dark green; but some shells are delightfully colorful, sporting bright green, orange, yellow, or red shading.

To make a turtle, provide each student with a 16-ounce paper soup bowl. Have each student color the outside of his bowl using black, brown, green, orange, yellow, and/or red markers. Next have each child trace around one of his hands on green construction paper and cut it out. Cut off the fingers and the thumb from the construction-paper hand at the palm. Staple the four fingers to the paper bowl to represent the turtle's feet. Cut a scrap from the remaining green paper and staple it in place to create the turtle's tail. Use a marker to add eyes and a mouth to the thumb; then staple it to the bowl to make the turtle's head.

Demonstrate to students how to bend the turtle's feet and head so it appears that the turtle is going into its shell. Then teach students the following song to sing as they move the turtle in and out of its shell:

### I'm A Little Turtle
*(sung to the tune of "I'm A Little Teapot")*

I'm a little turtle with a shell.
I have four legs, a head, and a tail.
When I get so scared I want to hide,
I pull my head and legs inside!

# Eager Beavers

This small-group construction activity will have your eager beavers chomping with excitement. Share *Busy Beavers* by Lydia Dabcovich (Scholastic Inc.) or *Beaver At Long Pond* by William George and Lindsay George (Greenwillow Books) with your students to help explain how beavers dam up streams to create ponds. Then have your students collect pebbles, sticks, and twigs. (Craft sticks can be substituted.) Place wet sand or dirt in a large, plastic tub and challenge a small group of students to build a beaver dam in the middle. When the dam is complete, test it to see if it will hold water. To test the dam, fill several 16-ounce cups of water and slowly pour the water behind the dam, one cup at a time. Did the dam hold? Continue the activity with additional small groups until each student has had a turn to help build a dam. To conclude the activity, ask students which type of construction worked best.

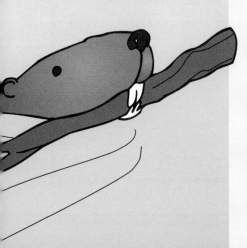

# Bookmark

Use with "Literature To Leap Over" on page 36.

Take the plunge...
Share a book with your child!

***Lily Pad Pond***
Written by Bianca Lavies
Published by Dutton Children's Books

***Jump, Frog, Jump!***
Written by Robert Kalan
Published by Greenwillow Books

***Splash!***
Written by Ann Jonas
Published by Greenwillow Books

***Do Not Disturb***
Written by Nancy Tafuri
Published by Greenwillow Books

***In The Pond***
Written by Ermanno Cristini & Luigi Puricelli
Published by Picture Book Studio USA

©1996 The Education Center, Inc. • *APRIL* • TEC248

# Parent Note

Use with "Ready To Explore?" on page 37.

## Dear Family,

We are studying pond life. We would like to make exploration kits to help us with our study. You can help us by sending in any of the following materials:

- resealable plastic bags (gallon and snack size)
- 3-oz. clear plastic cups
- plastic spoons
- yarn

Thank you for contributing to your child's learning!

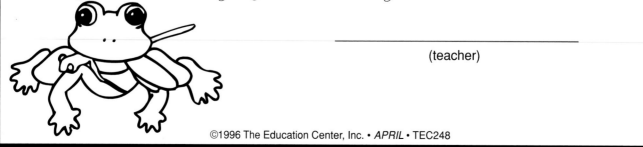

_____

(teacher)

©1996 The Education Center, Inc. • *APRIL* • TEC248

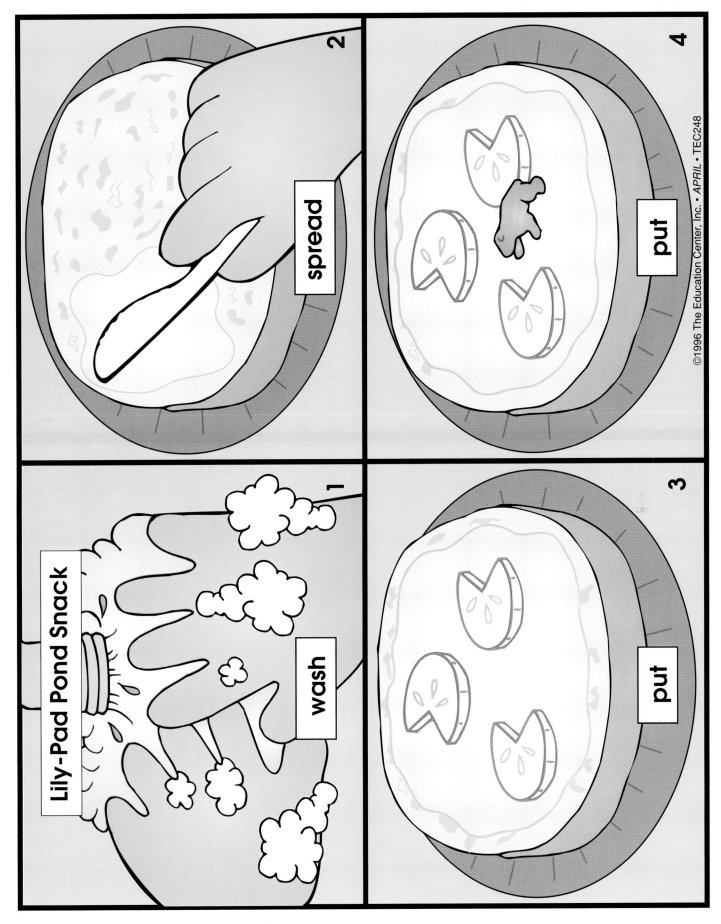

# My
# Pond Life
# Journal

By _____

©1996 The Education Center, Inc. • *APRIL* • TEC248

# My
# Pond Life
# Journal

By _____

©1996 The Education Center, Inc. • *APRIL* • TEC248

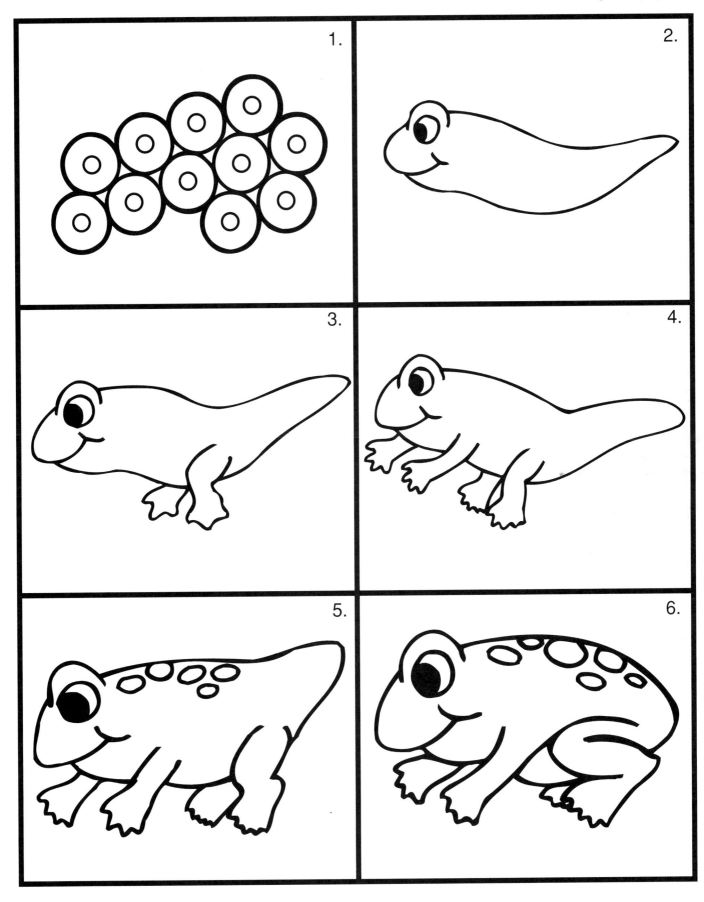

1.

2.

3.

4.

5.

6.

# READY, SET... LET'S GO!

Transportation keeps our world on the move. Whether for work or for play, transportation is an integral part of our everyday lives. Gear up with the following activities and take your youngsters on a trip through the curriculum using transportation as your guide.

*by Angie Kutzer*

## WHAT'S A VEHICLE?

Children usually know the labels *car, truck, plane, train,* and *boat,* but do they know that all of these objects are *vehicles*? Explain to your students that a vehicle is a means of carrying or transporting something. Label the top of a piece of chart paper "Vehicles We Know." List a few examples of vehicles and have your little ones tell what each named vehicle carries or transports. Then add to the list the names of other vehicles as suggested by the group. Read Anne Rockwell's *Things That Go* (Puffin Books) and complete the list with the names of any other vehicles your students want to add.

## AIR, LAND, OR WATER?

You'll need red (air), green (land), and blue (water) markers to take your youngsters to new heights—and depths—with this classification activity. Inform your little ones that there are three main types of transportation: air, land, and water. Revisit the vehicle chart that was made in "What's A Vehicle?" After each vehicle name, direct a child to write an *A, L,* or *W* with the corresponding colored marker to note how that vehicle travels. Have your students count the vehicles for each group as you make tally marks; then determine which type of transportation includes the most vehicles.

Vehicles We Know

tractor L        rocket A
ship     W       bike L
skateboard L     car L
plane A          jet ski W
train L          motorcycle L
jet A            glider A

*Barry Slate*

# OH, NO! A TRAFFIC JAM!

Your little traffic cops will practice their sorting skills during this traffic disaster. To prepare for this activity, duplicate and send home the parent note on page 55 with each student. Label each of five sentence strips with a different category—"cars," "planes," "boats," "trains," and "others." Glue a corresponding vehicle picture to each strip. (For the "others" group, glue on pictures that represent a variety of other forms of transportation.) You will also need a whistle.

Start the activity by having each child show his vehicle and tell how it is used. Then direct him to put his vehicle in the middle of the group. Once everyone has had a turn to share, blow your whistle and point to the pileup. It's a traffic jam! Arrange the category cards around the pile. Invite each child, in turn, to pick a vehicle from the pile and place it near the correct category card. Give him a happy toot for a correct response or a low, lingering blow for a signal to try again. Continue until the traffic jam is cleared.

For added fun with your students, count the number of vehicles in each category and determine which group has the most vehicles and which group has the fewest. Or make a pattern using the toy vehicles and challenge a student volunteer to extend it.

# LARGE-MOTOR LOCOMOTION

Your youngsters will rev up their engines as they perform the motions in this vehicle rhyme.

| | |
|---|---|
| Boats tug. | *(Hands reach forward and pull imaginary rope toward body.)* |
| Trains chug. | *(Knees alternately bend and straighten while arms are bent and rotate at side.)* |
| Planes fly. | *(Turn a half circle with arms lifted at sides.)* |
| Skates glide. | *(Feet slide on floor to complete circle.)* |
| Jeeps bump. | *(Bounce up and down.)* |
| Trucks dump. | *(Hold arms out to the front with palms up as if holding something; then drop hands and arms back down.)* |
| Rockets blast. | *(Squat down and jump straight up.)* |
| Cars go fast! | *(Hold hand flat at shoulder level with palm facing down; then quickly extend hand out in front of body.)* |

# WHEELS

## WONDERFUL WHEELS

Before the wheel, people had to carry their loads on their backs or use animals to transport heavy burdens. Wheeled vehicles revolutionized transportation by making it easier to move cargo and transport larger and heavier loads. Demonstrate this advancement with a set of encyclopedias or other large books and a luggage carrier. Have a student volunteer walk back and forth in front of the class as you stack books in her arms. When the load gets too heavy, direct her to set it on the floor and have the class count the books in the stack. Then give the child a luggage carrier and instruct her to push it back and forth across the room while you stack books again. When this gets too heavy, direct her to stop and have the group count again. Do wheels make a difference?

### THE "WHEEL" WORLD

Keep on rolling with the "wheel-ization" that wheels are everywhere. To prepare for this activity, duplicate page 52 for each child. Lead your little ones on a voyage in and around your school or center after asking them to count the number of wheels they see. Read aloud the story *Bumper To Bumper: A Traffic Jam*, by Jakki Wood (Simon & Schuster Books For Young Readers). After the story, use the endpapers to review the different wheeled vehicles. Distribute a wheel pattern to each child and instruct her to illustrate a wheeled vehicle or find, cut, and glue a picture of a wheeled vehicle from a magazine onto the wheel pattern. Fill in the blank with the vehicle's name; then have each child cut her wheel from the paper. Display these "wheel-ustrations" for all to admire.

### ALL ABOARD...THE FRIENDSHIP TRAIN

Play Jim Valley's "Friendship Train" (Rainbow Planet) and chug around the room with your youngsters. Choose a volunteer to be the engineer. Have the engineer move around the room and tap a friend to join him (by touching the engineer's shoulders). Then have the second child tap a friend to hook up to the friendship train. Continue until all of the children are winding around the room. Lead the train of little ones over to the circle-time area for a discussion of what makes a good friend.

Finish the activity by making this simple friendship train to display. Trace and cut each child's handprint from colored construction paper. Add two black construction-paper wheels to each handprint and cut out an engine shape. Attach all of the pieces along a wall, cabinet, or bulletin board. This train will remind your little ones that your classroom is a room full of friends!

# WIND

## MY TRIP ON A PLANE

Have any of your students taken a trip by airplane? Give them an opportunity to share their experiences with the group. Were they excited, nervous, or scared? Did they travel with their families or alone? If possible, take your little ones on a field trip to a nearby airport. Most larger airports have guides and special educational tours available. If a trip to the airport is not an option, share a factual book such as *Going On An Airplane* by Fred Rogers (Family Communications Inc.) with your youngsters. (This book is out of print. Check your local library.) After the story, head outdoors with your little ones and distribute balsa-wood airplanes for some free-flying explorations.

## HIGH-FLYING MATH

After some free-exploration time with their airplanes in the "My Trip On A Plane" activity, your children will soar with these math activities. To prepare, you will need a skein of yarn, scissors, and a large bull's-eye made from bulletin-board paper. Have each child, in turn, throw his plane. Measure the flight distance with yarn. Cut the length from the skein and hand it to the child. When everyone's plane trip has been measured, compare the lengths of yarn to see whose plane took the longest journey. For added fun, lay the bull's-eye near the group and have them try to land their planes in its center. Are there any budding pilots in your class?

Name Maria

## PLANE PARTS

Now that your little ones are frequent flyers, provide them with more information about the different parts of an airplane with the book *Let's Fly From A To Z* by Doug Magee and Robert Newman (Cobblehill Books). Duplicate page 54 and the flaps on page 55 for each child. Read the story (or paraphrase it for younger students); then assist your children in making their own lift-the-flap airplane models. Have each child cut out the flaps , then tape the tops of the flaps over the correct places on the plane pattern. These planes are sure to land on refrigerators all over town!

# WATER

## A BUNCH OF BOATS

Use the poem below with the flannelboard pieces on page 53 to expose your students to a variety of sailing vessels. Duplicate page 54 for later use; then cut out the boats on page 53. Laminate the pictures for durability; then attach a piece of felt to the back of each boat. Read the poem aloud and point to the specific boat as it is described. When your children are familiar with the rhyme, have volunteers place the correct boat on the board as you describe it. Anchors aweigh!

## BOATS, BOATS, BOATS

Look in the harbor.
What do you see?
Boats, boats, boats!
Count...one, two, three.

Here is an oil tanker bringing
  in some crude.
Here is a dinghy if you're in a
  sailing mood.

This ocean liner is the place to
  vacation,
Cruisin' through the waters all
  around our nation.

Boats, boats, boats!
Count...one, two, three.
In the big harbor,
Lots of boats to see.

## WHAT SANK THE BOAT?

The topic of boats and water transportation serves as a great springboard for exploring the scientific concepts of *sink* and *float*. Give your little ones a chance to estimate what it would take to sink the boat in this activity. In advance obtain an aquarium tank or other large, clear bowl; a small, plastic food container (the boat); and several different sets of manipulatives. You will also need to prepare a chart labeled as shown. To begin the activity, fill the large container with water and set the plastic boat afloat. Record several volunteers' estimations of how many pieces from one set of manipulatives it will take to sink the boat; then test the waters! Do this again with different sets of manipulatives, making sure that each child gets a turn to estimate at least once. Leave this experiment out for more exploration during free time. Think sink!

| What Sank The Boat? | | | | | | | | |
|---|---|---|---|---|---|---|---|---|
| | bear counters | | pattern blocks | | marbles | | crayons | |
| Jim | 8 | 12 | | | | | | |
| Amy | 3 | 12 | | | | | | |
| Lisa | 7 | 12 | | | | | | |
| Tommy | | | 10 | 13 | | | | |
| Daniel | | | 2 | 13 | | | | |
| Casey | | | 25 | 13 | | | | |
| Beth | | | 11 | 13 | | | | |
| Jasmine | | | | | 10 | 6 | | |
| Tyrone | | | | | 5 | 6 | | |
| Tabitha | | | | | 40 | 6 | | |
| Kate | | | | | 6 | 6 | | |
| Michael | | | | | | | 10 | 15 |
| Tosha | | | | | | | 10 | 15 |
| Kirby | | | | | | | 20 | 15 |

## MAKE IT FLOAT

Challenge your little shipbuilders to create floating vessels from balls of clay. Give each child a ball of clay and ask her to test it at the water table to see if it floats. Then encourage her to manipulate the clay and test it again. Have her continue molding and testing the clay until she has a worthy vessel. Reward the efforts of your first-rate mates with a snack of fish-shaped crackers.

## Bon Voyage!

End your trip into the world of transportation with this collaborative collage. Prepare the mural by taping three labeled strips of bulletin-board paper together as shown. Have your children paint, cut from magazines, or draw pictures of transportation vehicles. Question each child about the vehicle in his picture and how it travels. Then apply glue and invite him to attach his vehicle picture to the correct strip on the mural. When the mural collage is finished, enjoy it with your children as you sing this transportation song.

## On The Go!

*(sung to the tune of "Row, Row, Row Your Boat")*
Trans-por-ta-tion
Has three types we know:
Wheels, water, and wind
Keep us on the go!

## Transportation Titles

*Flying*
Written by Gail Gibbons
Published by Holiday House, Inc.

*The Big Red Bus*
Written by Judy Hindley
Published by Candlewick Press

*The Train Ride*
Written by June Crebbin
Published by Candlewick Press

*Freight Train*
Written by Donald Crews
Published by Greenwillow Books

*I Love Boats*
Written by Flora McDonnell
Published by Candlewick Press

*Flying*
Written by Donald Crews
Published by Greenwillow Books

*Sail Away*
Written by Donald Crews
Published by Greenwillow Books

*Tractor*
Written by Craig Brown
Published by Greenwillow Books

## Transportation Tunes

"Wheels On The Bus"
"Row, Row, Row"
Sung by Raffi
*Rise And Shine;* Troubadour Records Ltd.
Available from Educational Record Center
To order call 1-800-438-1637

"Riding In An Airplane"
Sung by Raffi
*One Light, One Sun;* Troubadour Records Ltd.
Available from Educational Record Center
To order call 1-800-438-1637

"Space Adventure"
Sung by Greg and Steve
*On The Move With Greg And Steve;*
Youngheart Records
Available from Educational Record Center
To order call 1-800-438-1637

"Rock-A-Motion Choo Choo"
Sung by Greg and Steve
*We All Live Together Vol. 1;*
Youngheart Records
Available from Educational Record Center
To order call 1-800-438-1637

"Let's Go Riding"
Sung by Red Grammer
*Can You Sound Just Like Me?;*
Red Note Records
To order call 1-800-824-2980

"Friendship Train"
Sung by Jim Valley
*Friendship Train;* Rainbow Planet
Available through The Wright Group
To order call 1-800-523-2371

**Wheel Pattern**
Use with "The 'Wheel' World" on page 48.

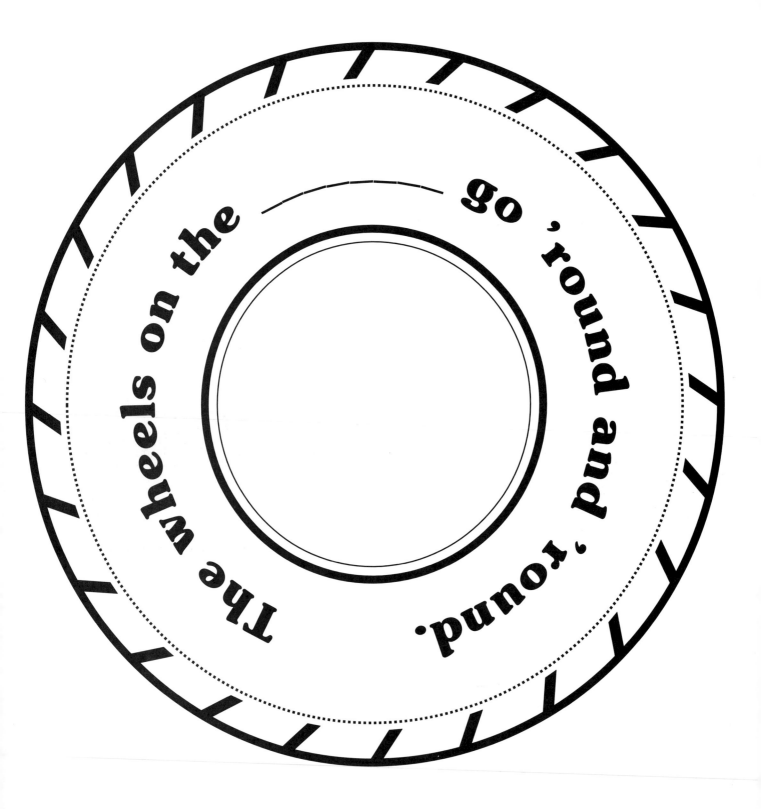

Name

cargo hold

cabin

fuel tanks

cockpit

**Note To The Teacher:** Use with "Plane Parts" on page 49.

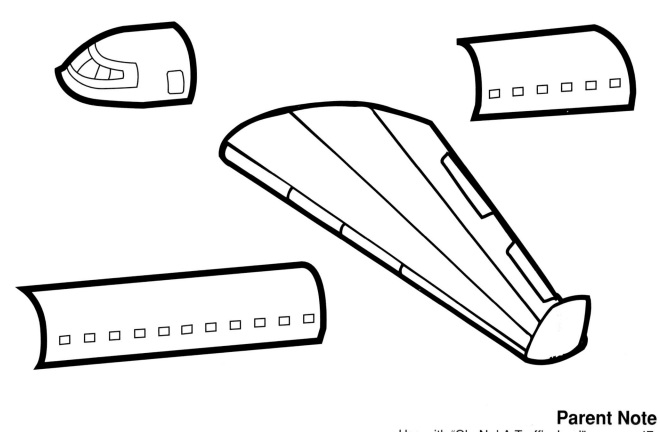

**Dear Family,**
We're revved up and ready to start our transportation unit! Please help me choose a toy vehicle to take to school tomorrow. My class will be using it for a high-performance sorting activity. Make sure that my name is taped to the bottom of my toy.

**Thanks for helping!**

# Here, Chicky, Chicky!

Youngsters delight in the sight of a soft, yellow chick. Encourage investigation and discovery with this coop full of chick activities.

*ideas contributed by Lori Kent and Angie Kutzer*

## An Extraordinary Introduction

Storytime is the perfect time to introduce this chick unit. Put a stuffed toy chick in a paper bag; then read aloud *An Extraordinary Egg* by Leo Lionni (Scholastic Inc.) You probably won't finish the story without hearing cries of, "That's not a chicken!" After the reading, put on your acting face and with a puzzled look, ask your little ones why they didn't think the baby alligator was a chick. Pretending not to know what a chick looks like, ask them to describe one for you. With an understanding grin, pull the toy chick out of the bag and inform your group that chicks will be the next unit of study. Peep! Peep!

## Plump Peepers

Your little ones will chirp with delight during this weighing activity. To prepare, fill several plastic eggs with different amounts of rice. Close each egg and tape around its seam to prevent the egg from separating. If desired, use paint pens to paint eyes and a beak on each egg. Have a student volunteer use a platform scale or a balance scale in order to weigh each egg. As each egg is weighed and compared, have a student sequence the eggs from heaviest to lightest. Leave the scale and eggs out for more weighing discoveries to be made during free time.

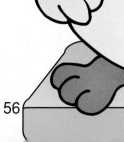

## All Cracked Up

Hand and shoe prints hatch some excitement in this art project! Give each pair of students two sheets of white and one sheet of yellow construction paper. Help them trace each other's hands onto the white paper. Then have each student trace the bottom of her partner's shoe onto the yellow paper. Instruct each child to cut out her own hand and shoe prints. Direct her to turn the shoe print upside down so that the heel is at the top; then have her draw eyes (or glue on wiggle eyes) and a beak on the heel part of the cutout. To make the egg, glue the handprint cutouts—palms touching and fingers out at the sides—to the bottom of the chick. Display these newly hatched chicks on a bulletin board titled "All Cracked Up!"

## Cheeper Sleeper

Encourage each of your youngsters to share his chick knowledge with his family by sending the stuffed toy chick from "An Extraordinary Introduction" on page 56 home for a sleep over. Put the chick in a straw-filled basket along with a journal, a favorite bedtime story, and some granola "chick feed" to share with its hosts. Attach a parent note to explain the activity and request that a page in the journal be written about the night's festivities. When the child and chick return the next day, read his journal entry to the class and invite him to share any other details about his sleep over. Your students will each be eager to be the next one who entertains!

## An "Egg-cellent" Story

A chick's development inside an egg is a fascinating, yet hard-to-explain wonder for little ones. *Egg Story* by Anca Hariton (Dutton Children's Books) provides an excellent explanation for you to share with your children. After the story, let your little cheepers dramatize hatching as you teach them the following song:

### The Chick In The Egg
*(sung to the tune of "The Wheels On The Bus")*

The hen on the farm lays a smooth white egg,
Smooth white egg, smooth white egg.
The hen on the farm lays a smooth white egg,
Cluck, cluck, cluck, cluck, cluck!

Inside the egg grows a little chick,
Little chick, little chick.
Inside the egg grows a little chick,
In twenty-one days.

The chick has a beak to crack the egg,
Crack the egg, crack the egg.
The chick has a beak to crack the egg,
Tap, tap, tap, tap, tap!

He hatches from the egg and flaps his wings,
Flaps his wings, flaps his wings.
He hatches from the egg and flaps his wings,
Flap, flap, flap, flap, flap!

The hen keeps her chick warm in the nest,
In the nest, in the nest.
The hen keeps her chick warm in the nest,
Peep, peep, peep, peep, peep!

# The Reading Nest

Invite your children to relax in the reading nest while enjoying a chick story from the list below. To create a nest, fill an inexpensive baby pool with raffia and a few white pillow "eggs." Complete the environment by sprinkling a few colored craft feathers around the nest. This nest will entice every youngster in the room over to check out some chicks in print.

### Books To Chirp About

*Birthday Chickens*
Written by Shirley Kurtz
Published by Good Books®

*The Chicks' Trick*
Written by Jeni Bassett
Published by Cobblehill Books

*Hatch, Egg, Hatch!*
Written by Shen Roddie
Published by Little, Brown and Company

*Here Comes Henny*
Written by Charlotte Pomerantz
Published by Greenwillow Books

*The Story Of Chicken Licken*
Written by Jan Ormerod
Published by Lothrop, Lee & Shepard Books

## Chick Chow

Your little chicks will love scratching and pecking for worms with this outside game. Make the worms ahead of time by bending brown pipe cleaners into curvy worm shapes. Then scatter the pipe-cleaner worms in a grassy area. Get a paper plate; then lead your class outside and divide them into small groups. Designate a certain number of worms for the groups to find. As a child finds a worm, have her run back to you and place it on the plate. On your signal, send one group at a time to "peck" for worms while the other groups count the worms that are placed on the plate. Be sure to have a bag of Gummy Worms® ready for the chicks who peck their way into a feeding frenzy!

## The Sky Is Falling!

Your chick unit won't be complete until you introduce your youngsters to that infamous chick, Chicken Licken. Add a hip-hop twist to this traditional tale by using the rap version "Chickey Lickey" found on the Once Upon A Rhyme collection by CJ & Friends. (This tape can be ordered through National Educational Network at 1-800-537-6647.) Toes will be tappin' and wings will be flappin' to this funky beat. After several playings of the song, have student volunteers pantomime along with the music. Duplicate the characters on page 60 onto construction paper for each child. Have your little ones color and cut out the animal pictures, then tape the pictures to craft sticks for their own puppet show—to the beat, of course!

## Chickie's Walk

This class-made big book will definitely be a group favorite! Read aloud the story *Rosie's Walk* by Pat Hutchins (Aladdin Books); then ask your students to recall some of the places Rosie visited. Emphasize any positional words that your children use to describe where Rosie walked. Inform your students that each of them will be illustrating a different place for Rosie's baby, Chickie, to visit. Give each child a piece of paper; then write her dictation as she tells you where the chick is walking. Remind her to use a positional word in her phrase. Staple the pages inside a simple, barn-shaped cover made from construction paper. Share the complete story of "Chickie's Walk" with your class.

## A "Cheep" Snack

Gather the following ingredients together in your cooking center and assist your little ones in making these chick treats. Purchase (or ask parents to donate) a package of Nutter-Butter® cookies, plastic knives or craft sticks, vanilla frosting (tinted yellow), candy corn, and chocolate chips. To make a chick, spread frosting over a cookie; then add two chocolate-chip eyes and a candy-corn beak. These goodies will end your chick unit with lots of peeps, cheeps, and mmmmmms!

# "Egg-cellent" Eggs

Pique your youngsters' curiosities as they crack open the mystery of what is inside an egg.

*ideas contributed by Linda Rice Ludlow*

## Discovering Eggs

Set the stage for your study of eggs by bringing in a basket filled with eggs (real or plastic) for your little ones to explore. Ask your young students to guess what's inside the eggs and then share their ideas with the group. Then read the book *Chickens Aren't The Only Ones* by Ruth Heller (Grosset & Dunlap) to show many animals that hatch from eggs. After discovering the different creatures that hatch from eggs, sing "Have You Ever Seen An Egg?" with your little ones. Encourage them to pantomime a snake, bird, or fish hatching as they sing the words to this creative song.

## Have You Ever Seen An Egg?

*(sung to the tune of "Have You Ever Seen A Lassie?")*

Have you ever seen an egg and thought, "What is inside it?"
Have you ever seen an egg and thought, "What is inside?"
It could be a snake or a bird or a "fishy."
Have you ever seen an egg and thought, "What is inside?"

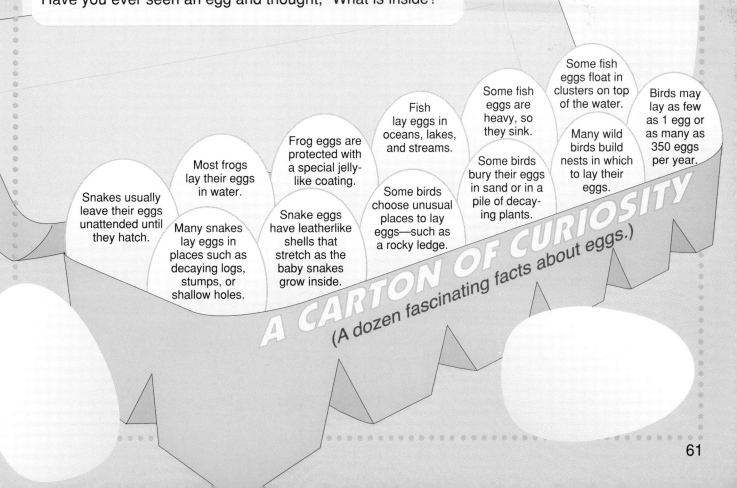

Snakes usually leave their eggs unattended until they hatch.

Most frogs lay their eggs in water.

Many snakes lay eggs in places such as decaying logs, stumps, or shallow holes.

Frog eggs are protected with a special jelly-like coating.

Snake eggs have leatherlike shells that stretch as the baby snakes grow inside.

Fish lay eggs in oceans, lakes, and streams.

Some birds choose unusual places to lay eggs—such as a rocky ledge.

Some fish eggs are heavy, so they sink.

Some birds bury their eggs in sand or in a pile of decaying plants.

Some fish eggs float in clusters on top of the water.

Many wild birds build nests in which to lay their eggs.

Birds may lay as few as 1 egg or as many as 350 eggs per year.

A CARTON OF CURIOSITY
(A dozen fascinating facts about eggs.)

## What's Inside?

Challenge your young students to do some creative thinking and drawing with this "egg-ceptional" project. Reread *Chickens Aren't The Only Ones* by Ruth Heller (Grosset & Dunlap) to review the many types of animals that hatch from eggs. Then have each student create her own version of an egg with an animal that's ready to hatch inside. For each student, duplicate the egg patterns on page 65. Ask each youngster to write her name on the line on the cracked eggshell. On the other egg, have her draw and color an animal that hatches from an egg. Next have each child cut on the heavy black lines, including the zig-zag line. Finally have each child put glue on the gray areas on the whole egg shape and place the two half-shapes on top as shown. Let the glue dry; then display all the eggs on a bulletin board, and have your little ones guess what's inside each egg. Encourage youngsters to open the two shell halves on each egg to satisfy their curiosities.

What Is Inside?

by Alyssa

## Keep It Under Wraps

Play this fun discovery game with your little ones, and watch the wonder in their eyes as they discover what you're keeping under wraps. To prepare for the game, locate a small stuffed animal that could hatch from an egg (such as a duck). Tightly wrap this animal in layers of colored tissue paper—alternating colors—creating an egg shape as you add each tissue-paper layer. Create enough layers to be equal to or more than the number of students playing the game.

Have your little ones sit in a circle; then show them the large, paper egg shape. Tell your students that a special animal is hiding inside and ask them to guess what animal it is. Give the egg shape to the student next to you, and have him unwrap one layer of the paper. Ask him to feel the animal and make a guess about its identity. Encourage him to tell one fact about the animal he guessed, if he can. Then have him pass the egg to the next student, who unwraps the next colored layer and takes a guess. Continue passing the egg until everyone has unwrapped a layer and taken a guess. Then slowly unwrap the few remaining layers and reveal the animal inside. Have your little ones stand if they guessed the animal correctly.

## Egg Habitats Hunt

Review the facts in "A Carton Of Curiosity" (page 61) and discuss the places where many animals lay their eggs. Often an animal can be identified by where its egg has been laid or placed. Set up a special egg hunt in your classroom to help your students identify some of these egg habitats. Partially hide plastic eggs in a variety of locations, such as the water table, the sand table, and an actual nest (or a nest created from raffia).

Then take students on a pretend nature hike to hunt for these eggs. Turn on your acting abilities as you guide students carefully through the murky waters of a pond, lead them up a steep mountainside and along a narrow cliff, and put on sunglasses as you near a sandy beach in search of hidden eggs. At each location, have your students discuss that habitat and what animal(s) might have laid eggs there. Your little hikers will enjoy the adventure and learn about animal habitats and likely nesting locations, too!

## Three Little Eggs

Share this charming, creative-movement poem with your youngsters as a fun review of counting skills.

| | |
|---|---|
| Three little eggs in the birdie's nest— | *Hold up three fingers.* |
| A lovely shade of blue. | *Cup hands together to form a nest.* |
| All of a sudden one did hatch; | *Throw arms up and out.* |
| Now there are only two. | *Hold up two fingers.* |
| | |
| Two little eggs in the birdie's nest, | *Hold up two fingers.* |
| Warming in the sun. | *Cup hands together to form a nest.* |
| All of a sudden one did hatch; | *Throw arms up and out.* |
| Now there is only one. | *Hold up one finger.* |
| | |
| One little egg in the birdie's nest, | *Hold up one finger.* |
| Missing all the fun. | *Cup hands together to form a nest.* |
| All of a sudden it did hatch, | *Throw arms up and out.* |
| And now look—there are none. | *Make a zero with one hand.* |
| | |
| No little eggs in the birdie's nest, | *Make a zero with one hand.* |
| As you can plainly see. | *Make binoculars with hands over eyes.* |
| Three little birdies sit and sing | *Hold up three fingers.* |
| High up in the tree. | *Hold hands above head and sway like a tree.* |

## Hatch, Hatch, Little Egg

Your little ones will be chirping for more after they participate in this marvelous movement activity. Involve your youngsters in some creative dramatics to share the sensations of a baby bird hatching from an egg. Ask each youngster to kneel down and curl into a ball shape, pretending to be in an egg. Then tap one student on the shoulder—signaling him to begin hatching. Have that student dramatize the process of tapping on and breaking out of the shell, testing his newfound wings, and uttering his first, "Tweet, tweet." Have this newly hatched little one tap another student in an egg; then continue play until everyone has hatched.

For a variation, try this activity while students sing "Have You Ever Seen An Egg?" (page 61). Encourage children to hatch as other animals, such as fish, tadpoles, or snakes.

## Edible Nests

Teach your little ones about nest building with this tasty activity. To prepare the nest-making material in advance, melt one 12-ounce bag of peanut-butter chips over low heat, add two 3-ounce cans of chow-mein noodles, and stir until noodles are thoroughly coated. Then spread the mixture on a cookie sheet and separate the clumps as much as possible. Let the mixture cool; then divide it into a class supply of small, resealable plastic bags. Before beginning the nest-building activity, hide these bags of noodle mixture in your classroom.

When you are ready to begin, explain to your youngsters that birds must search for the materials they need to build their nests. Tell each youngster to begin searching for "dried grass" and "straw" to build a nest, and show an example of the bagged mixture that your little ones will actually find. Instruct each student to find one bag, then return to the work area where the nest construction will take place. At the work area, give each child a plain donut and some chocolate frosting to use as mud. Have each student use a plastic knife to spread the frosting on his donut and then top it with the grass mixture. Lastly give each child some candy eggs or jelly beans to place in his nest. Share the book *A Nest Full Of Eggs* by Priscilla Belz Jenkins (HarperCollins Publishers) while your little ones enjoy their treats.

Hannah

## Bird's Nest Art

Extend your youngsters' nest-building technique by including this creative, textured art project. First gather materials—such as raffia, straw, yarn, or string—and cut them into short pieces. (If weather permits, take the children outside to collect natural items.) Next give each student a sheet of white construction paper. Ask each student to put a large ring of glue on her paper. Then have her apply pieces of the nest-building materials to the glue to create a nest shape. Lastly have your little ones add the final touch—the eggs. Have each child carefully dip her thumb into a small amount of tempera paint, then press thumbprints in the center of her nest to represent eggs. Let the glue and paint dry; then display the final creations in your classroom or hallway for all to admire.

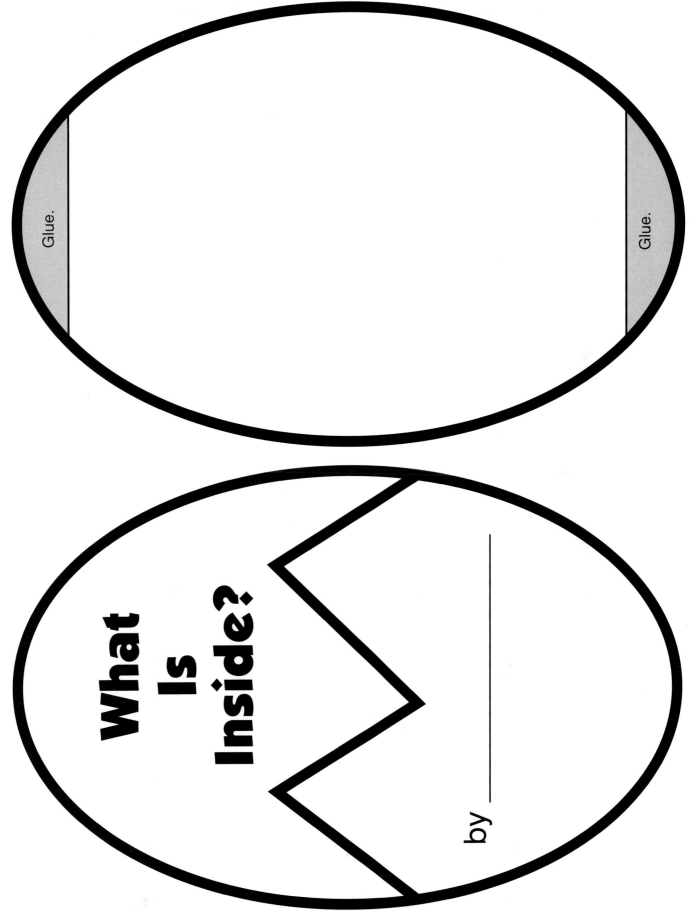

What
Is
Inside?

by _____

# Taking Care Of Our Earth

The environmental concerns that launched the first Earth Day on April 22, 1970, continue to be today's concerns as we work to nurture our Earth back to health. Use these multidisciplinary activities to awaken your youngsters' awareness of ecological issues and to motivate them to take action in helping to restore our planet.

*ideas contributed by Carrie Lacher and Mackie Rhodes*

## Sharing Nature

Capitalize on each child's curiosity and fascination with nature by making it a part of his daily environment—and promote an appreciation and respect for the earth in the process! In advance prepare a nature center with some magnifying glasses, measuring devices, a scale, paper, writing utensils, and a display area. For each child, duplicate the parent request letter on page 73; then laminate each letter for durability. Put the letter in a large, resealable storage bag labeled with the child's name. Each week send the bag home with the child. When he returns his nature item to school, invite him to place it in the nature center. If desired, write his dictated description or name of his item on a notecard and place the card with his item. Each time the child brings a new nature item to school, have him replace the item he brought previously. Encourage youngsters to make regular visits to the nature center to investigate the items on display. Engage them in discussions about the items and invite them to illustrate some of their discoveries. It's a natural fact—youngsters are fascinated by nature!

## The Earth And I Are Friends

Introduce youngsters to a dear friend—Earth! To begin show students a globe. Explain that the globe represents Earth and its many different geographical features—such as land, oceans, mountains, and deserts. Invite a volunteer to help you locate your school's approximate location on the globe. If desired, mark that spot with a smiley-face sticker. Then read aloud *The Earth And I* by Frank Asch (published by Harcourt Brace & Company). Afterward ask youngsters to describe some ways in which they are friends with Earth. Can they name some things that make Earth sad? Happy? Write each student's response about an Earth-friendly activity on a small sheet of note paper. Then use a smiley-face sticker to attach each note to a large bulletin-board-paper cutout decorated to resemble Earth. Display the cutout with the title "Friends With The Earth."

66

# Earth Is Our Friend...So What's The Problem?

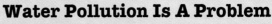

Pollution is the problem. Help youngsters begin to understand how pollution harms the earth with these concrete experiences.

## Air Pollution Is A Problem

Our air is made dirty—or *polluted*—by the harmful gases that come from many factories and vehicles. Help students see what dirty air can do to a beautiful Earth with these polluted-air projects. In advance mix equal amounts of baby powder and dry, black tempera paint in a plastic container to create a gray powder. Have each child draw a nature scene—such as mountains, a farm, or a beach—on a sheet of white construction paper. Then, while outdoors, attach each child's picture to a fence or wall. Give each child a plastic spoon partially filled with the gray powder. Explain that the mixture represents air pollution; then instruct her to hold the spoon at mouth level, holding the bowl of the spoon close to her picture. Have her gently blow across the bowl of the spoon so that the powder blows onto her picture. After she has blown all the powder from the spoon, invite her to examine her nature picture to determine how it was affected by air pollution. Afterward invite students to shake the pollution off their nature scenes, then take the pictures home to share with their families.

## Water Pollution Is A Problem

Our rivers, lakes, oceans, and seas are polluted by garbage and numerous chemicals. Youngsters can observe firsthand what happens to living things when they are exposed to polluted water with this demonstration. Partially fill two clear plastic cups with water. Remove the tip of an old black marker with tweezers and put it in one of the cups to simulate polluted water. Then place the cut end of a celery stalk (with leaves) into each of the cups. Allow the stalks to stand undisturbed for several hours, inviting youngsters to periodically check them for any changes. What changes do they observe? What is causing the changes? Ask students to brainstorm some ways in which they can help keep water sources in their community clean.

## Acid Rain Is A Problem

When gases from air pollution get into rain clouds, *acid rain* falls from the clouds instead of clean, pure rain. Over time, acid rain can harm all growing things. Invite youngsters to experiment with plants and simulated acid rain to discover the negative impact acid rain has on our environment. Have students help you plant grass seed in two large plant trays. Label one grass garden "Clean Rain" and the other "Acid Rain." After the seeds begin to sprout, have students water the "Clean Rain" garden with a spray bottle filled with tap water and the "Acid Rain" garden with a solution of two parts vinegar and one part water. Compare the two gardens daily. Ask youngsters to describe the differences they observe between the gardens.

## Earth Walk

Now that youngsters have some understanding of the pollution problem, guide them to identify problems on their section of Earth during an investigative outdoor tour. In advance cut out shapes to resemble a tree and a trash can from separate sheets of bulletin-board paper. Display these cutouts near your group-time area.

While on your Earth walk, encourage youngsters to point out things that are a natural part of the outdoors—such as leaves, rocks, and sticks. Also have them identify things that are not part of nature—such as discarded paper, cans, and bottles. After returning to the classroom, ask students to list some of the things they observed while on their Earth walk. Write each response on the cutout that best represents the observation—the tree for things that belong in nature or the trash can for things that do not belong or are harmful to nature.

## Let's Talk Trash!

Youngsters will be amazed to learn that each of us generates approximately four pounds of trash a day! But just how much is four pounds of garbage? To demonstrate, place an empty trash can on a bathroom scale. Have students put paper, empty containers, and other throwaway items in the can until the scale reaches four pounds. Invite each child to lift the can to feel the weight of the garbage. As an extension, have her find an object in class that weighs about the same as the garbage. Ask her to put that item in a large box. After every student has added her item to the box, challenge youngsters to try to move or lift the box. Is it heavy or light? Explain that one person's trash may not seem to be very much, but when a group of people combine their trash, it amounts to a lot.

To help students learn how to decrease the amount of trash they generate, read *Where Does All The Garbage Go?* by Melvin Berger (Newbridge Communications, Inc.). After discussing the book and things that can be recycled, have youngsters help make the containers described in "Stop, Think, Recycle!" on page 69; then encourage them to begin their class trash reduction/recycling program immediately.

# Stop, Think, Recycle!

Since little ones now know that they can help reduce the amount of trash they make, invite them to help set up a recycling center right in their own classroom. For more recycling information and ideas, read aloud *Recycle! A Handbook For Kids* by Gail Gibbons (Little, Brown and Company); then have students discuss the many ways they can contribute to a class recycling effort. Then divide your students into three equal groups. Have each group decorate a separate box to use as a recycling container—one for paper, one for plastics, and one for aluminum cans. Label each box to indicate the type of materials it will contain; then hot-glue a few sample items onto that box. Place the boxes in a designated recycling area of the classroom. As youngsters make trips to the trash can, encourage them to consider whether their throwaway items might be recyclable. If so, have them put each item in the appropriate container. Empty the filled containers into your school's recycling bins. Or, if possible, arrange a class trip to a local recycling facility to deposit the class recyclables there. Continue your class recycling project throughout the school year.

As an extension, you might arrange for volunteers and parents to send in a variety of clean recyclable products made of paper, plastic, and aluminum. Challenge small groups of students to sort these products into the appropriate recycling containers.

## From Trash To Treasure

Imaginations will run free when youngsters get their hands on a collection of recyclable and reusable free craft items. And by reusing items, they will be contributing to an Earth-friendly activity—reducing trash. Simply gather a large assortment of items, such as plastic containers and lids, plastic soda bottles, magazines, cardboard, Styrofoam® packing pieces, and six-pack rings. (Be sure to thoroughly clean all containers.) Add some traditional craft items to the collection, too—such as wiggle eyes, pom-poms, craft sticks, pipe cleaners, glue, and scissors. Then invite your little ones to create away!

## Helping Out—The Three Rs

Summarize how each of us can help make Earth a cleaner place to live with these three words—reduce, recycle, and reuse. Explain each of these terms to students, giving a few examples of each. Then teach youngsters the hand motion shown for each term. Invite them to sing this song, performing the hand motions each time the three Rs are mentioned.

### Reduce, Recycle, Reuse
*(sung to the tune of "Three Blind Mice")*

Reduce, recycle, reuse.
Reduce, recycle, reuse.

Now's the time to choose.
There must be no excuse.

It's up to each one of us to do
Our part to make the Earth clean, it's true.
So let's work together—yes, me and you!

Reduce, recycle, reuse.

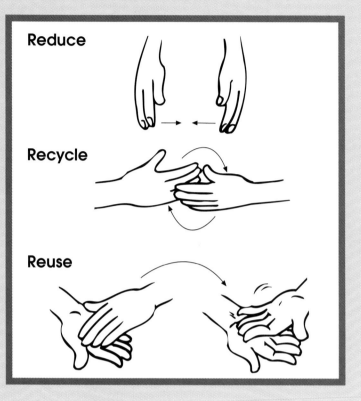

Reduce

Recycle

Reuse

**Reduce, Recycle, Reuse**
*(sung to the tune of "Three Blind Mice")*

Reduce, recycle, reuse.
Reduce, recycle, reuse.

Now's the time to choose.
There must be no excuse.

It's up to each one of us to do
Our part to make the earth clean, it's true.
So let's work together—yes, me and you!

Reduce, recycle, reuse.

## Earth-Friendly Families

Attract and hold the attention of your students and their families with these child-made magnetic reminders to participate in Earth-friendly activities. In advance duplicate the Earth pattern on page 72 on tagboard for each student. Also duplicate the song pattern on page 73 and the family letter on page 74 for each child. To make a magnet, have each child cut out his Earth and song patterns. Have him sponge-paint the Earth cutout with blue and green tempera paint. After the paint dries, instruct the child to glue the song onto his Earth cutout. Attach a strip of magnetic tape to the back of each child's cutout. Read a copy of the family letter to students; then have each child take home a copy of the letter with his magnet. Encourage youngsters to teach their families the song and to remind them to do their part in making our Earth clean.

## Banding Together

Youngsters will identify with one another in their environmental efforts when they wear special armbands during Earth-friendly class projects. For each child, duplicate the armband pattern on page 75 on a sheet of tagboard. Have the child cut out her pattern; then invite her to embellish her cutout with her choice of boldly colored markers or glitter crayons. To make the armband, punch a hole near each corner of the cutout. Thread a separate length of narrow elastic through each hole on one side of the armband; then thread each piece of elastic through the hole on the opposite end of the band. Fit the armband to the child's arm and securely tie the elastic. Encourage each youngster to wear her armband during projects such as those described in "Pick A Project."

## Pick A Project

Keep little ones continuously aware of the need to take care of our Earth by planning regular Earth-friendly projects. After obtaining permission from your school administrators, guide your class in selecting an area to "adopt" for scheduled cleanups. Or have students participate in seasonal projects such as planting in the spring, collecting paper trash from other classrooms after holiday celebrations, or making bird feeders from reusable items in the winter. Each time the children participate in an Earth-friendly project, invite them to wear their armbands made in "Banding Together."

## Earth-Friendly Reading

*Kids For The Earth*
Written by Melvin Berger
Published by Newbridge Communications, Inc.

*This Is Our Earth*
Written by Laura Lee Benson
Published by Charlesbridge Publishing

*For The Love Of Our Earth*
Written by P. K. Hallinan
Published by Ideals Children's Books

*The Lorax*
Written by Dr. Seuss
Published by Random Books For
  Young Readers

*The Great Trash Bash*
Written by Loreen Leedy
Published by Holiday House, Inc.

# Earth Pattern

Use with "Earth-Friendly Families" on page 70.

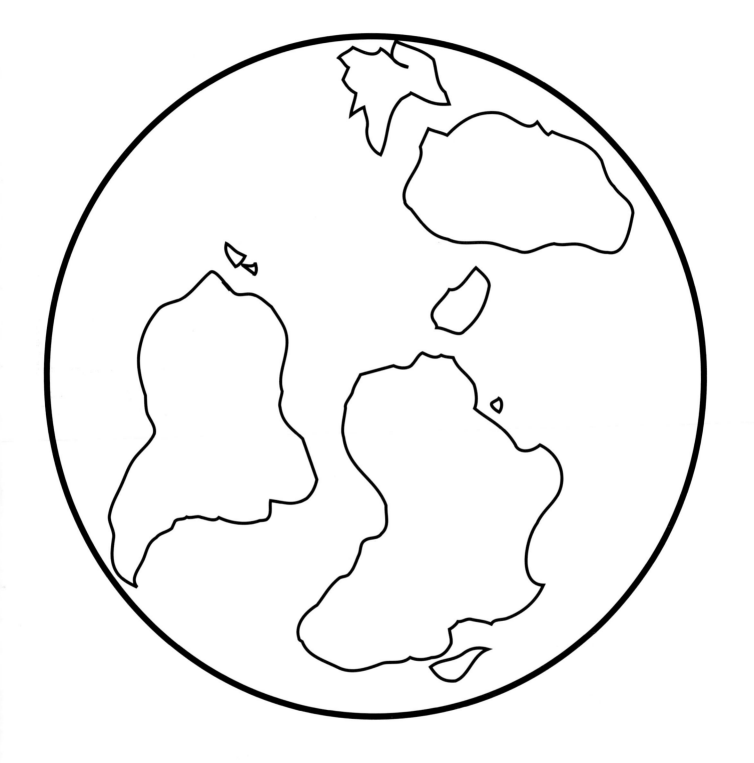

Dear Parent,

Exploring and investigating things of nature is one way to help our children develop respect and appreciation for our Earth. As part of our study on Earth Day, it is requested that your child bring in an object of nature to include in our nature collection. Each week please take a little time to explore the outdoors with your child in search of an item to send to school—a pinecone, leaf, feather, unusual rock, or some other item. During your explorations, please be careful not to disturb the creatures and growing things in nature! Enclose the item in the bag provided and return the bag to school. Your child will have the opportunity to tell about the item and to add it to our collection.

Your cooperation and support in your child's education is always appreciated!

_____
(teacher)

©1996 The Education Center, Inc. • *APRIL* • TEC248

### Reduce, Recycle, Reuse
*(sung to the tune of "Three Blind Mice")*

Reduce, recycle, reuse.
Reduce, recycle, reuse.

Now's the time to choose.
There must be no excuse.

It's up to each one of us to do
Our part to make the Earth clean, it's true.
So let's work together—yes, me and you!

Reduce, recycle, reuse.

## How To Grow An Earth-Friendly Family

Plant each heart firmly in the fertile soil of care.
Help clean our Earth completely—the water, land, and air.
Work faithfully together—as a group, solo, or pair.
Be creative. Be fun-loving. Be Earth-friendly with a flair!

### Earth-Friendly Things To Do:

• Reduce the use of paper products in your home. Use items such as washable dishes, cloths, and handkerchiefs instead.

• Set up recycling containers in your home. Recycle paper, aluminum, glass, and plastics. If you don't have curbside pickup of recyclables in your area, deposit them at your local recycling center regularly.

• Reuse as many items as possible. For instance, take paper or plastic bags with you to use on shopping trips. Or sterilize and reuse glass juice jars in which to refrigerate water or powdered drink mixes. Use emptied diaper-wipe boxes for small-object storage. The possibilities for reusing items are endless!

• Organize, or participate in, group outings to pick up litter and clean up parks, beaches, roadsides, and other public-use areas.

• Plan a special project or put forth extra effort to contribute to the care of our Earth on Earth Day, April 22—plant a family tree, participate in a neighborhood cleanup, or have a yard sale.

EARTH'S FRIEND

EARTH'S FRIEND

# Ants All Around

If your little ones are always stopping on the sidewalk to observe the antics of a group of ants, then they'll love these activities. So get busy and go buggy!

*by Ada Hanley Goren*

## Get The Facts

There's no better way to begin a unit on ants than by observing the real thing. So take your youngsters on a search for ants outside your classroom. Chances are, it won't be long before they encounter a parade of ants on a sidewalk or a grassy playground, because ants live almost everywhere. Caution students not to touch the ants. Some types can bite or sting! Encourage your students to watch for a while and comment on the ants' appearance and actions. Then return to your classroom.

Share a factual book about ants, such as *Ant Cities* by Arthur Dorros (Scholastic Inc.) or *The World Of Ants* by Melvin Berger (Newbridge Communications, Inc.). The second book can be ordered directly from Newbridge at 1-800-867-0307.

Then share some more fascinating facts about ants with your curious crew:

- There are more than 9,000 kinds of ants!
- Ants have been on Earth since before the days of the dinosaurs.
- Different types of ants make different types of homes. Some live under the ground, some live inside wooden twigs, and some even "sew" leaves together to make nests.
- Ants are very important to people. They eat other insect pests, scatter seeds, and stir up the soil, which helps plants and forests grow.

## Model Ants

Like all insects, ants have three body parts, six legs, and two antennae. Show students a close-up photo of an ant (from an encyclopedia or a factual book), and point out these features. Then invite youngsters to make ants from clay. Provide each child with some modeling clay, one-half of a coffee-stirring stick, and eight short lengths of pipe cleaner. Ask each youngster to divide her modeling clay into three pieces and roll each piece into a ball. Have her push the balls onto the stirring stick to make the three body parts of her ant. Then have her poke six short lengths of pipe cleaner into the center ball to create the ant's six legs, as shown. Encourage her to add two pipe-cleaner antennae to finish her model ant.

If desired, prepare a large, simple drawing of an anthill on a sheet of bulletin-board paper. Lay the paper on a large table or on the floor, and invite youngsters to move their clay ants around on it.

## Ants Up Close

Your little ones will enjoy observing ants in a *formicarium*—an ant farm! Purchase one at your local science store, keeping in mind that you usually have to order the ants by mail. Or—if you're adventurous—make an ant farm in a large jar. To begin, fill a widemouthed jar with sifted dirt. Gather some ants in a separate jar, being careful to avoid ants that sting or bite. Add the ants to the dirt-filled jar. (Do this outdoors in case some get away!) Then lay a small piece of damp sponge and some food for the ants—such as a small piece of bread or some potato-chip crumbs—on top of the dirt. Cover the top of the jar with a piece of a nylon stocking secured with a rubber band. Wrap and tape a piece of black construction paper around the jar.

Place the completed ant farm in your science center. Periodically remove the black paper so students can observe the ants' activities. Keep the sponge damp and replenish the food as necessary. Release the ants after a week or two, near the area where you found them.

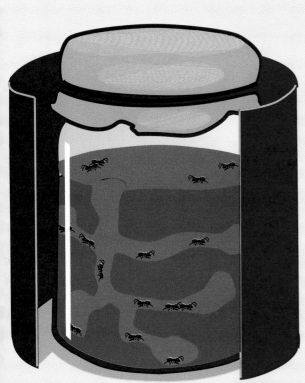

## Anthill Art

After their observations, your students will be ready to illustrate anthills full of busy ants with this finger-painting technique. At a table, provide each child in a small group with a dollop of brown finger paint on a vinyl placemat. Have him smear the paint over the placemat. Then encourage him to finger-paint the tunnels and rooms of an anthill. Have some illustrations—such as those in *Ant Cities* (see "Get The Facts" on page 76)—available for inspiration. When each child's anthill is finished, lay a sheet of white construction paper over his painting, press down lightly, and lift it up. Voilà—an imprint of his finger-painted design! Allow the prints to dry; then provide ant stickers or copies of the ant patterns on page 82, so that students can add ants to their anthills. As students finish their artwork, ask each child to dictate to you something he has learned about ants. Write his dictation on a sentence strip. Mount each child's anthill and statement on a bulletin board for an "ench-ant-ing" display!

Ants keep food in their nests.

## Edible Anthills

Your little ones will want to dig into this tasty snack! Gather the necessary ingredients, utensils and supplies (see below), and prepare the recipe cards on page 83. Duplicate page 84 for later use. Then remove page 83 and glue it to a sheet of tagboard. Laminate it for durability, if desired; then cut apart the cards. Invite each child to follow the steps on the recipe cards to prepare an edible anthill. Yum!

### Edible Anthill

**Ingredients For One:**
1 graham cracker
several chocolate-covered
 raisins (ants)

**Utensils And Supplies:**
1 resealable plastic sandwich bag
1 clear plastic cup
1 plastic spoon

## If You Were An Ant,...

There are three types of ants in a colony—a *queen,* a few *males,* and thousands of *workers* (all female). A queen's only job is to lay eggs that will grow into new ants. A male's only job is to mate with the queen. All the rest of the work is done by the worker ants. Ask children to imagine that they are worker ants—members of a large, busy colony. Share the different types of jobs available to worker ants:

**Nurse:** cares for eggs and larvae
**Construction Worker:** digs new rooms and tunnels and carries dirt outside
**Hunter:** goes in search of food and brings it back to the nest
**Security Guard:** defends the nest against enemies

Then ask each child to vote for the job he'd like to have if he were a worker ant. Prepare a class graph to show the results. Label four index cards with the four job titles, and place the cards in a pocket chart, as shown. Give each child an index card and ask him to write his name on it. Have him add some ant art to his card as follows: Ask him to press a fingertip onto a red or black stamp pad, then onto his card three times to make three connected ovals representing an ant's body. Provide fine-tipped markers so he can add legs, antennae, and facial features to his ant. Then ask each child to add his card to the pocket chart, beside his choice of job. Give each child a chance to explain his decision. Be sure to discuss the concepts of *more, fewer,* and *equal* as you count the votes.

## A Cooperative Colony

Ants are *social* insects, which means they live and work together in groups called *colonies.* Try this activity to teach your students about the social life of ants and encourage classroom cooperation as well. Read the classic story *"I Can't," Said The Ant* by Polly Cameron (Scholastic Inc.). Then lead a discussion about how the ants in the story cooperated to get the job done and how real ants cooperate for the good of their colony.

Guide your youngsters in this cooperative activity. Ask one student to pick up your desk or a heavy table and move it to another location in the classroom. When the child is unable to accomplish this task alone, guide students to see that a group effort will be necessary. Encourage your students to work together as a cooperative colony at other jobs, such as cleanup time.

| Sugar | Butter | Seeds | Cereal |
|-------|--------|-------|--------|
| Angie | Kathy | Jerry | Sue |
| Matt | Sally | Mike | John |
| Ruth | | | Clevell |
| Billy | | | Bobby |

## "Ant-icipation"

Give youngsters an opportunity to anticipate the actions of their neighborhood ants with this fun experiment. Begin by asking students the question "What do ants like to eat?" You'll probably get a wide variety of answers. Actually different kinds of ants like to eat different things—ranging from insects to seeds to sweets. Find out what the ants that live near your school or center like best with this experiment.

Fold a large sheet of paper into fourths. On each section, put a different food: *sugar, butter, sunflower seeds,* and *cereal.* Then label a bulletin-board-paper chart as shown. Tell students that you will place the four foods outside your classroom. Ask each youngster to sign her name or place a name card in the column under the food that she thinks the ants will like best. Leave the paper with the foods outdoors overnight or during the school day; then encourage students to examine it closely. Ask students "Which food do our neighborhood ants prefer?"

For additional prediction practice, have students carefully observe the path taken by the ants to get to the paper. After a day or two, put only the favorite food out again. Have students predict—by signing their names on a yes/no chart—whether they think the ants will take the same path again.

## Finding Food

Demonstrate the teamwork that ants use to bring food back to their nests with this game. To prepare, fill two picnic baskets each with 15 or more plastic foods from your housekeeping area. Divide your class into teams of five children each. Two teams at a time may play. For fun, designate one team as the Red Ants and the other as the Black Ants for each game. In a large open space, designate a separate area to serve as each team's nest. Place the picnic baskets side by side—an equal distance from both nests.

To play, each team begins in its nest. One ant from each team crawls to his team's designated basket and removes one piece of food. He then crawls back to his team's nest, carrying the food under his chin to imitate the way an ant carries food in its jaws. That child then makes a second trip to the basket—this time accompanied by the second team member, who may also return with one piece of food. The game continues by adding one more ant on each trip, until one team has emptied all the food from its basket into its nest.

## Like Ants To A Picnic...

Your little ones will be attracted to this fun and "a-maze-ing" activity! Duplicate page 82 for each child. Have her cut out the individual ants at the bottom of the page. Help her tape a paper clip to the back of one ant. Have her place this ant at the start of the maze; then show her how to hold a small magnet on the underside of the paper and make the ant "crawl" along the path toward the picnic. Encourage students to use the mazes individually or hold ant races with others!

79

## Ants On The Move

Create an army of ants in your classroom when you invite youngsters to make ant headbands. First cut several individual cardboard egg cups in half, as shown. Each half-cup will create a set of ant's jaws. Along with an egg-cup half, provide each child with a four-inch circle of construction paper, a pipe cleaner cut in half, and two large sticky dots. Have each child peel the backing off the dots and stick them to the paper circle to represent her ant's eyes; then have her tape the pipe-cleaner halves to the back of the circle and bend them to resemble antennae. Have her glue the jaws in place as shown. Then help each child glue her finished ant face to the center of a sentence strip. After the glue has dried, adjust each child's completed headband to fit her head and staple the ends in place.

Once they're wearing their ant attire, invite youngsters to march around your room to a recording—or your own rendition—of the classic tune "The Ants Go Marching." Challenge your students to march in single file, in pairs, in trios, and in quartets, as dictated by the verses of the song.

## Ants In Your Pants? Dance!

Teach youngsters this rhyme that invites the circle-time sillies! To prepare for this activity, duplicate an ant pattern from page 82. Color the pattern and laminate it for durability. Then seat your students in a circle and teach them the verse below. Once they're familiar with the rhyme, begin passing the ant cutout around the circle. Have each child place the ant cutout on the named piece of clothing (or whatever he is wearing that is closest to it) as the ant is passed to him. Encourage the child who receives the ant on the last line "Ants in your pants? Get up and dance!" to hop up and perform his own creative dance—with all the wiggles and jiggles he desires! Repeat the verse as many times as desired.

Ants in your hat? Imagine that!
Ants in your shirt? Oh, does it hurt?
Ants in your sweater? It could be better.
Ants in your sock? How do you walk?
Ants in your shoe? Oh no, poor you!
Ants in your pants? Get up and dance!

Amazing Ants

by Breyanna May

Ants have Six legs
1

nts live Underground
2

Ants can Carry food in their jaws
3

## Amazing Ants

Are your little ones getting antsy to show off their knowledge? Duplicate the booklet cover and pages on pages 84–85 for each child. Have each student cut apart his booklet cover and pages, stack the pages in order under his cover, and staple them together at the left edge. After writing his name on his booklet cover, invite each student to dictate an ending for the sentence on each page to demonstrate what he knows about the appearance, habitats, and activities of ants. Then invite him to illustrate his sentences. Encourage your little ones to take their finished booklets home to share with their families.

## An "Ant-thology" Of Ant Books

*Two Bad Ants*
Written by Chris Van Allsburg
Published by Houghton Mifflin Company

*One Hundred Hungry Ants*
Written by Elinor J. Pinczes
Published by Houghton Mifflin Company

*Amazing Anthony Ant: A Flap, Maze, Song, And Search Book*
Written by Lorna & Graham Philpot
Published by Random House, Inc.

*Step By Step*
Written by Diane Wolkstein
Published by Morrow Junior Books

*Effie*
Written by Beverley Allinson
Published by Scholastic Inc.

*The Ant And the Elephant*
Written by Bill Peet
Published by Houghton Mifflin Company

# Maze And Ant Patterns

Use with "Anthill Art" on page 77, "Like Ants To A Picnic..." on page 79, and "Ants In Your Pants? Dance!" on page 80.

Find the path that leads the ant to the picnic.

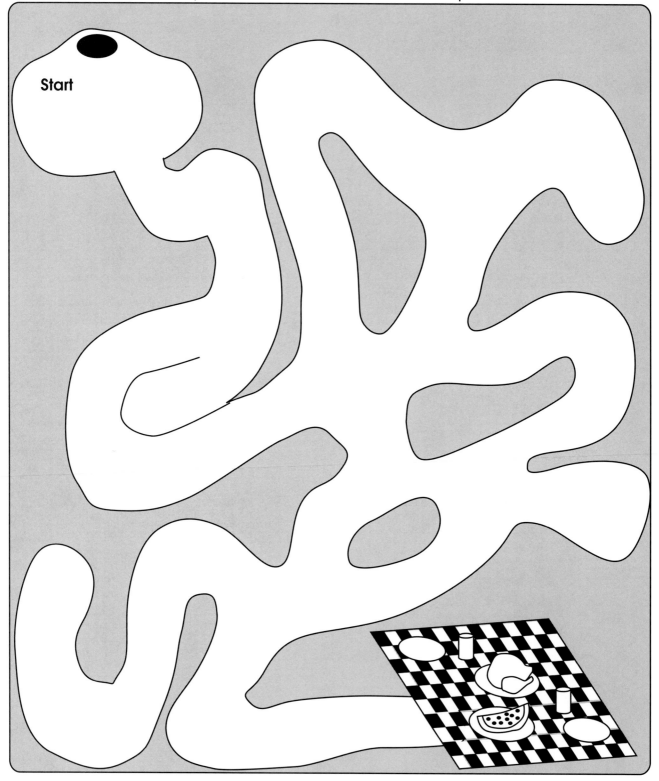

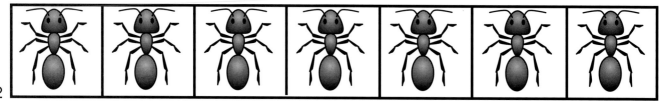

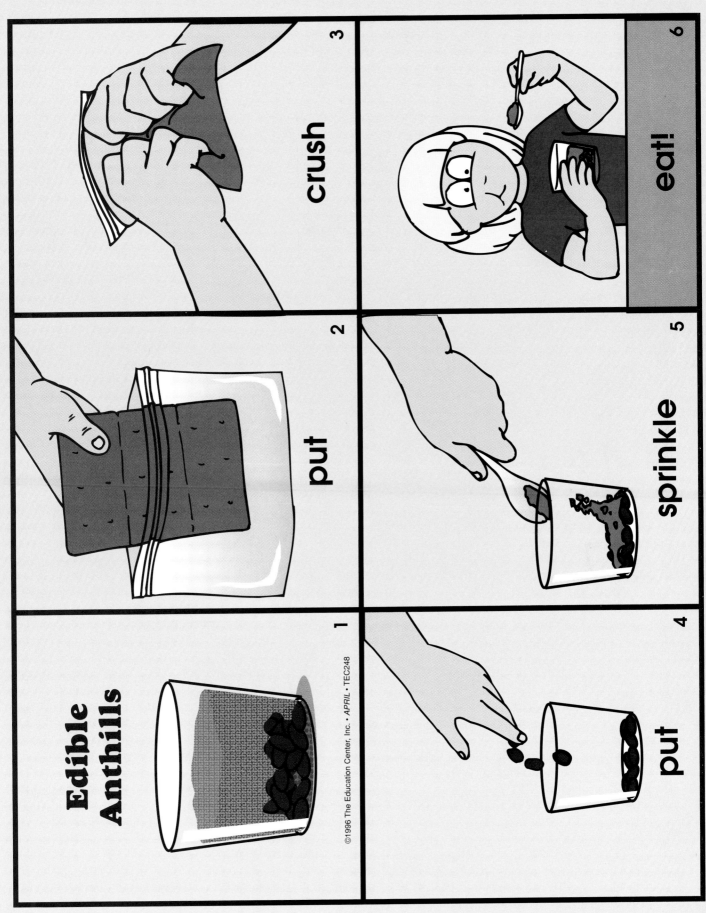

Edible Anthills

crush

put

put

sprinkle

eat!

©1996 The Education Center, Inc. • APRIL • TEC248

# Booklet Cover And Page

Duplicate before using page 83. Use with "Amazing Ants" on page 81.

Amazing Ants

by

Ants have _____.

1

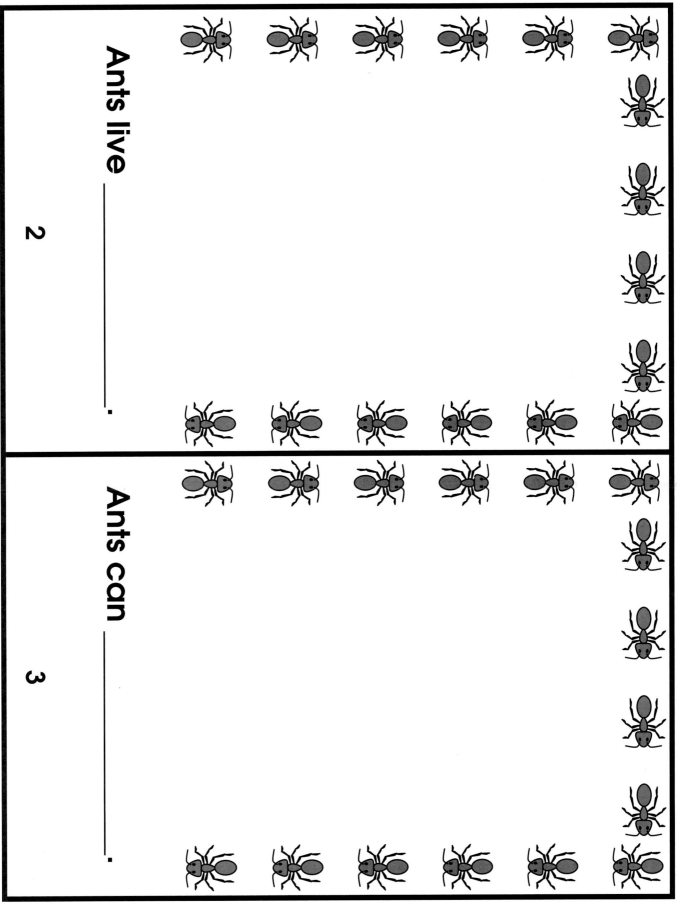

Ants live _____.

2

Ants can _____.

3

# Baby Animals

All baby animals grow. All baby animals change.
Some baby animals' bodies might even rearrange.
Some babies are adorable. Some really look quite strange.
The ideas in this unit provide youngsters with the range.

*ideas contributed by Lucia Kemp Henry and Mackie Rhodes*

## In The Beginning

Students will be eager to tell about their own growth and changes when they are introduced to the life changes experienced by a variety of animals. Share the picture sets and text of the animal sections of *Watch Them Grow* by Linda Martin (Dorling Kindersley) or *My First Book Of Nature: How Living Things Grow* by Dwight Kuhn (Scholastic Inc.). After examining each picture set, encourage students to discuss the ways in which the animal showed change and growth. Then guide youngsters to describe some ways in which they have changed since infancy. Conclude the discussion by requesting that each child bring a set of two or three photos to school—each showing the child at a different age in his life. Display the photo sets on a bulletin board with the title "We All Change And Grow."

## All Animals Change And Grow

Reinforce the concept that all animals change and grow with this simple song. If desired, give each child a picture of a different animal; then group your class into pairs of students. Have each pair in turn replace the underlined words with the two animal names represented by their pictures. For a variation, invite the student pairs to sing their own names, instead of the animal names, in the appropriate lines of the song.

*(sung to the tune of "London Bridge")*

Animals all change and grow,
Change and grow, change and grow.
Animals all change and grow,
Just like me!

[Cats] and [dogs] all change and grow,
Change and grow, change and grow.
[Cats] and [dogs] all change and grow,
Just like me!

Repeat the song as many times as desired, replacing the underlined words with a different set of animal names—such as *cows* and *horses,* or *ducks* and *chickens.*

# From Egg To Animal

Fascinate your little ones with the knowledge that every animal starts as a tiny egg. In advance duplicate page 94 for future use; then mount the animal sequence cards on page 93 on a sheet of tagboard, cut them apart, and laminate the cards for durability. Attach the hook side of a piece of Velcro® to the back of each card. Then explain to students that some animals grow inside their parents' bodies while other animals grow and hatch from eggs outside of their parents' bodies. To demonstrate the growth of animals that hatch from eggs, show the picture sets for the frog, butterfly, turtle, and duck in *My First Book Of Nature: How Living Things Grow* by Dwight Kuhn (Scholastic Inc.). Or use the flannelboard sequence cards prepared for this activity. Discuss the changes shown in the pictures for each animal. Then invite small groups of youngsters to take turns sequencing the cards for each animal on the flannelboard.

# Naming The Baby

Youngsters will enjoy reciting this rhyme about baby animal names. To prepare the flannelboard figures for this activity, duplicate page 96 for future use; then mount the animal patterns on page 95 on tagboard. Cut out and laminate each picture for durability. Attach the hook side of a piece of Velcro® to the back of each cutout. As the class recites the rhyme, have a different volunteer place the animal mentioned in each verse on the flannelboard.

Here is a baby.
Its wobble makes you laugh.
This baby cow
Is a darling little *calf.*

Here is a baby.
Its short tail has a curl.
This baby pig
Is a *piglet* boy or girl.

Here is a baby.
It's so frisky and bright.
This baby horse
Is called a *foal,* that's right!

Here is a baby.
It's furry and fluffy.
This baby dog
Is a cute little *puppy.*

Here is a baby.
Its white wool is so neat.
This baby sheep
Is a *lamb,* so very sweet.

Here is a baby.
It's playful through and through.
This baby cat
Is called a *kitten,* it's true.

Here is a baby
Its home is in the water.
This baby duck
Is a *duckling* son or daughter.

Here is a baby.
It's quite perky and quick.
This baby chicken
Is a cute and fuzzy *chick.*

# Taking Care Of Baby

Many animal parents take care of their babies in some way or another—even if only for a brief period of time. Read aloud *Animals And Their Babies* by Melvin Berger (Newbridge Communications, Inc.) to find out how some animals care for their young. Then invite students to play some of these games that incorporate baby animal caretaking in the fun.

## Feed The Little Birds

The ways in which baby animals get their food varies from one animal to another. Baby birds, or *fledglings*, rely on their parents for food. The fledglings sit in their nests with their enormous mouths gaping wide so that they can be fed. Encourage youngsters to practice counting and making comparisons while they play this bird-nest game. To prepare, place several large plastic hoops of different colors on the floor to represent bird nests (or label each hoop with a different-colored sticker). Assign a different child to role-play the parent bird for each nest. Give each parent a package of Gummy Worms® and have her stand a distance from her nest. Then randomly give each of the other students—or fledglings—a colored plastic chip to correspond to the color of one of the nests.

On a signal, have all the baby birds go to their appropriate nests. Encourage the fledglings to hold their palms together near their mouths, and to open and close their hands to resemble bird beaks. Instruct each parent bird to feed each fledgling in her nest by placing a worm in its beak. Then have the fledglings in each nest stand up in turn so that the parent bird can count them. Encourage the parents to compare the number of fledglings in each nest. Then invite the babies to eat their food. Repeat the game, inviting a different group of children to be the parent birds.

## Warm Bunnies

Different animals protect their babies in different ways. A mother rabbit keeps her rabbit *kittens* warm by covering them with dried grass. Give youngsters an opportunity to explore size and spatial concepts when they role-play rabbits in this game. To prepare, place a Hula-Hoop® on the floor to represent a rabbit's nest. Put three stacks of towels—hand towels, standard-sized bath towels, and oversized towels—to the side. From a group of four students, invite one child to role-play the mother rabbit. Have the other students role-play rabbit kittens moving around to some "hoppin' " music. Stop the music; then have the babies curl up in the nest. Encourage the mother to cover her babies with towels from one of the stacks. When the babies are completely covered, ask the mother to remove the towels one at a time as she counts them. Then ask her to pick another stack of towels with which to cover her babies. Will she need more or fewer towels of this size? Encourage her to compare the number of towels needed of each size to completely cover her kittens. Then invite another child to role-play the mother rabbit in the same fashion.

## Carrying Cubs

Baby animals get from place to place in a variety of ways. The mother lion carries each of her young babies—or *cubs*—by grasping the loose skin on the back of the cub's neck with her teeth. Invite students to group into lion families with this color-match and counting game. To begin, provide four or five construction-paper color choices from which each child may choose to make a simple lion-cub headband. Make an additional headband of each color to use for the mother lions.

To play, invite a different child to role-play the lion mother for each color headband represented. Have her wear the extra headband, instead of her own, as she assumes the role. Encourage the other children to wear their cub headbands as they perform lionlike actions to some lively music. After a brief period of time, stop the music. Instruct each lion mother to find her cubs by the color of their headbands. Have the mother "transport" each of her cubs to a designated home by loosely holding the back of the child's shirt and guiding him in the appropriate direction. After all the cubs are gathered, ask the mother lion to count the cubs in her family. Then repeat the game, inviting a different group of children to role-play the mother lions.

## Fishing Lessons

Many animal parents must spend time teaching their young how to survive. The bear teaches its babies—also called *cubs*—how to catch fish. In this matching game, youngsters will delight in role-playing bears that target and catch just the right fish! In advance cut out an equal number of large and small fish shapes from sheets of craft foam. Pair each large cutout with a small cutout; then label the front and back of each set with a matching shape, design, or number. Or label each large cutout in a set with a different uppercase letter and the small cutout with the corresponding lowercase letter.

To play, partially fill your water table or a small, plastic swimming pool with water. (You may prefer to play this game outdoors.) Put the fish sets in the water; then divide your class into pairs of students. Have each partner in a pair assume a role as a bear—the parent or the cub. Encourage the bear parent to "teach" her cub how to catch a fish by using her paws to capture a large fish. Then have the parent show the fish to her young and invite her baby to catch the small fish labeled with the corresponding skill. Have both bears compare the fish to check for a match. After several turns, invite the partners to switch roles; then continue the game until all the matches are found. Return the fish to the water and invite another pair of students to play the game in the same manner.

# A Child's Play Is A Lesson To Learn

In the world of young animals, play is one way that many lessons are learned. Offer youngsters some play opportunities related to baby animals and provide them with valuable practice in curriculum-related skills.

## Baby Talk

Puppets and toy animals add the playful touch needed to reinforce the names of young animals and the sounds they make with this rhyme. Invite a different volunteer to hold a toy model or puppet of each animal. When the animal is mentioned in the rhyme, encourage the child holding that animal to manipulate it as if it is responding to the question. Or, if desired, place each figure prepared in "Naming The Baby" on page 87 on the flannelboard as that animal is mentioned in the rhyme.

Mother [Duck], Mother [Duck],
What does your baby say?

"My little [duckling]
Says '[quack, quack]' all day!"

Each time the rhyme is repeated, replace the underlined animal names and sound with the corresponding words in one of the following sets:

*Cow, calf, "moo"*
*Pig, piglet, "oink"*
*Horse, foal, "neigh"*
*Dog, puppy, "woof"*
*Sheep, lamb, "baa"*
*Cat, kitten, "mew"*
*Chicken, chick, "peep"*

## Sand Booklets

Create a booklet at the sand table? Why not? Invite each student to visit the sand table to create her own textured baby-animal booklet to share with her family. In advance prepare several containers of sand of different colors—red, blue, green, or any colors of your choice. To make colored sand, mix dry tempera paint with sand until you achieve the desired color. Place the containers of colored sand near the sand table. For each child, duplicate the booklet cover and pages on pages 92, 94, and 96 on white construction paper. Have each child cut apart her booklet pages, write her name on the cover, and color the pictures on each page. Then have her trace the numbers on the booklet pages with glue. Invite her to place the pages, one at a time, in the sand table and sprinkle some of the colored sand over the glue to create raised numbers. Have her shake the excess sand into the sand table. After the glue dries, have each child cut out the cover and booklet pages; then help her staple them together in order. Encourage each student to take her booklet home to share with her family. For additional fun, pour the remaining colored sand into the sand table; then invite small groups of students to take turns engaging in some colorful sand play.

**Two** little piglets have snouts that wiggle.

## Animal Baby Buddies

Invite little ones to create their own animal baby buddies to enhance their dramatic play. To make an animal buddy, join two Styrofoam® balls together with a toothpick and glue as shown. After the glue dries, have the child paint the body with tempera paint. After the paint dries, invite the child to add details—such as wiggle eyes, construction-paper ears, and pipe-cleaner legs and a tail—to complete his animal. Encourage youngsters to use their animal buddies in the dramatic-play area.

## Tiny Baby Birds

Create lots of these baby birds in an assortment of colors for students to use in their manipulative activities and dramatic play. To make a baby bird, glue two bead or sequin eyes and construction-paper feet and a beak onto a pom-pom to resemble a bird. Place the birds in a center; then invite youngsters to use the birds in creating color patterns or in color-matching activities—such as placing each bird in a nest cut-out or plastic egg of the same color. Or have students practice counting out the number of birds to place in correspondingly labeled baskets. Put some of the baby birds in the dramatic-play area, and encourage children to incorporate them into their imaginative play. Invite youngsters to use the pom-pom creatures in other activities as well—after all, these activities are for the birds!

## Books About Baby Animals

*Lullaby Babes*
Written by Maribeth Boelts
Published by Albert Whitman & Company

*One Hungry Baby: A Bedtime Counting Rhyme*
Written by Lucy Coats
Published by Crown Publishers, Inc.

*Baby's Book Of Animals*
Written by Roger Priddy
Published by Dorling Kindersley

*Amazing Animal Babies*
Written by Christopher Maynard
Published by Alfred A. Knopf, Inc.

# My Baby Animal Book

**by** _____

©1996 The Education Center, Inc. • *APRIL* • TEC248

**One** little lamb has wool so white, four shaky legs, and eyes so bright.

©1996 The Education Center, Inc. • *APRIL* • TEC248

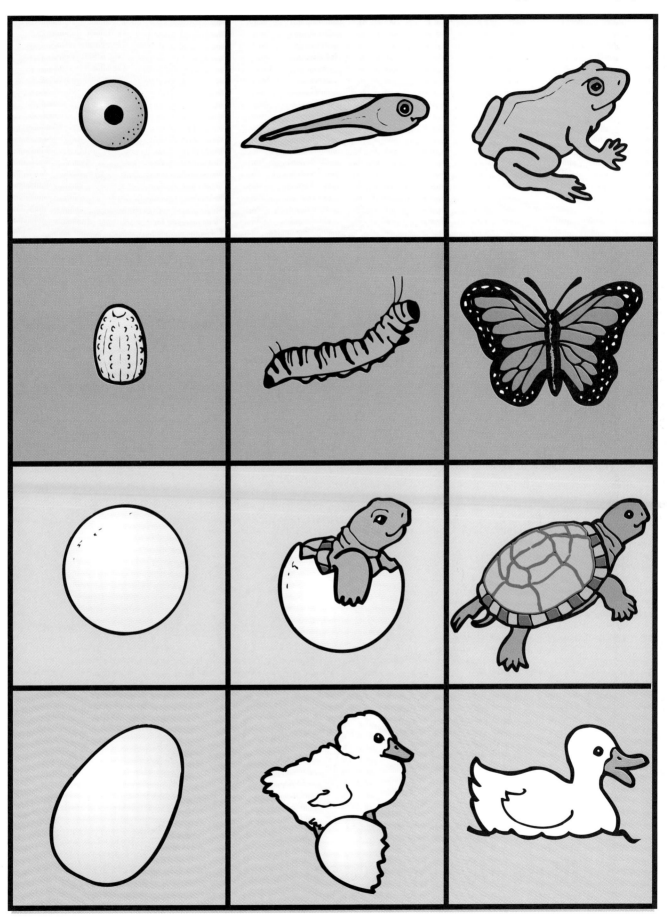

**Two** little piglets have snouts that wiggle.

**Three** little puppies have coats that tickle.

95

**Four** little kittens have faces so sweet.

**Five** little ducklings have little webbed feet.